T0381157

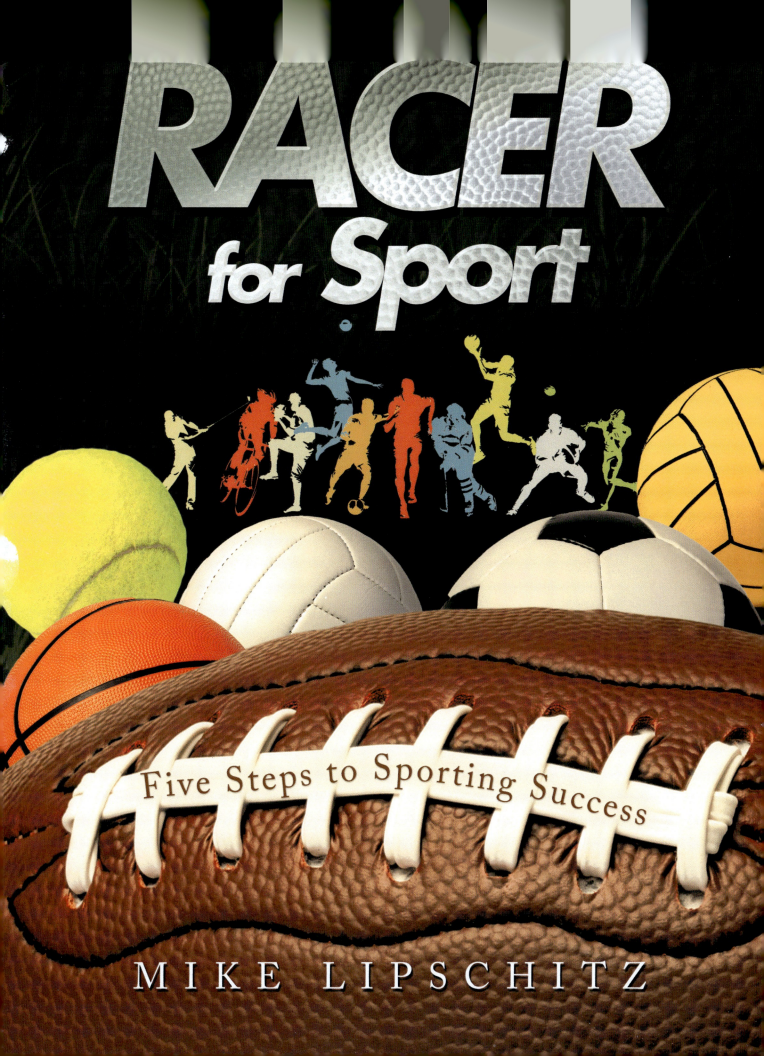

RACER
for Sport

Five Steps to Sporting Success

M I K E   L I P S C H I T Z

DEDICATION

A massive and sincere thank you to pupils past and present and my family and friends, without whom this book wouldn't have happened. And to Melissa Good, my amazing editor. And especially to Jytte Simmons, for her incredible patience, time and encouragement to help get this book out.

Learn more about Mike at mikestennis.com

AuthorHouse™ UK
1663 Liberty Drive
Bloomington, IN 47403 USA
www.authorhouse.co.uk
UK TFN: 0800 0148641 (Toll Free inside the UK)
UK Local: 02036 956322 (+44 20 3695 6322 from outside the UK)

Because of the dynamic nature of the Internet, any web addresses or links contained in this book may have changed since publication and may no longer be valid. The views expressed in this work are solely those of the author and do not necessarily reflect the views of the publisher, and the publisher hereby disclaims any responsibility for them.

Any people depicted in stock imagery provided by Getty Images are models, and such images are being used for illustrative purposes only.
Certain stock imagery © Getty Images.

Mike Lipschitz asserts the moral right to be identified as the author of this work.
A catalogue record of this book is available in the British Library.

Editorial and Production: Melissa Good, Jytte Simmons, Georgia Good
Illustrations: Hannah Simon
Photos: The Mike Lipschitz Collection

Every effort has been made to trace copyright holders, and the author apologises for any unintentional omission

Find out more about Mike at mikestennis.com

This book is printed on acid-free paper.

ISBN: 978-1-7283-5296-1 (sc)
ISBN: 978-1-7283-5295-4 (e)

Print information available on the last page.

Published by AuthorHouse 12/02/2020

authorHOUSE®

Contents

ABOUT MIKE

*"Clown: Let sense and reason, love and passion have
their say. But let us have a bit of fun as well."*
– GOETHE, *FAUST*

After many years of prompting from fellow professionals, pupils, family and friends, I have finally decided to commit over four decades of love, experience, knowledge and expertise to pen and paper.

To arrive, it has taken 42 years of coaching experience and thousands of Mike's Tennis Academy pupils, including over 250 students who have since undertaken full and part-time coaching qualifications, to affirm RACER as crucial to their improved understanding, enjoyment and matchplay performance.

The combined encouragement and acknowledgement of world-class coaches in various sports and across several countries helped me to get this unique concept out to the broader public. I am very fortunate to be based in Cambridge in the United Kingdom, with its wonderful intellectual history, which has given me access to advice and discussions, as well as to bounce ideas off world-renowned professors and lecturers testing the intellectual accuracy and efficacy of the system, which I am proud to say has stood the rigours of analytical examination.

Added to these formidable calls came the nudging, nodding, cajoling and unwavering belief and support of my close family and friends.

The more I have thought about sport and the more I have watched, taught, discussed and played numerous sports, the more convinced I am that this is the right time to present the breakthrough RACER system formally to the public at large.

At the same time, having observed and trained hundreds of assistants as well as coaches, I am very excited that, as a bonus in this book, I introduce the acronym 'SELF', which is a truly fantastic foundation for any coaching relationship. I believe that if the principles in SELF are followed, properly understood, and integrated into the individual's environment, it will make an enormous impact. The response from the echelons of Cambridge Academia as well as many other sources has been incredible.

Above all, it has taken innumerable hours of tried and tested work to ensure that the RACER system you are about to discover will improve your game and coaching, no matter what sport you play, and at any level of proficiency or excellence.

In this regard, I include para athletes. High level para sports first took off in 1948 and reached a pinnacle at the London 2012 Summer Paralympics, with full stadiums of over 80,000 people, as well as other venues, sold out. The achievements and skills of these athletes are brilliantly documented in the 2020 film *Rising Phoenix*. The point here is my wish to have these athletes use my system. I have included some para examples in this book.

The same efficacy of the system applies for coaches. The result is that I hope RACER will heighten your enjoyment of the games you love to play, coach or watch, as it has done for so many others.

My success in the sports industry, latterly in tennis, is due to a unique blend of knowledge, determination, creativity, experience, enthusiasm, academic proficiency and perhaps, above all, an impassioned desire to make learning and playing enjoyable for all.

I was raised in South Africa as a privileged white person with sporting and academic opportunities hard to match anywhere in the world. I received private tuition in the sports I played. My parents also put no limits on my academic pursuits – though there is not much discussion about which I spent more time on, and enjoyed success in. I mention this to illustrate the blend of sporting proficiency and analytical, intellectual competency that I was fortunate to acquire. This combination has allowed me to write a book of this type, offering knowledge, experience and analytical acumen when it comes to sport.

I sometimes walked a thin line growing up during the Apartheid regime. My small, personal involvement in opposing Apartheid elements through education and sport is something I look back at with pride. There might be another book on this someday!

Sport is an incredible means of breaking down barriers and I knew this instinctively from an early age. In 1977, my father's best friend, Joe Pamensky, then President of the South African Cricket Union, helped wrangle the government's permission for our league's cricket teams to play in the townships. This was at a time when sport was segregated and African, Indian and so-called 'Coloured' people had extremely limited access to any sports and all within the confines of their segregated area outside the main white towns.

Few white people ever went to the townships and a bunch of white adults and kids playing cricket in places like Lenasia township was a radical move. It proved to be an immensely transformative personal experience.

I'll also never forget my mouth erupting in fire from my first experience of a 'mild' curry in Lenasia, an Indian township outside of Johannesburg. We went for lunch at our Indian opposition's houses, as they had no fancy cricket pavilion like ours for lunch.

As a funny aside, rather than individual cricket fields with boundaries, as is usual, we played on a vast terrain of five pitches. Once one of my friends needed the toilet and off he was driven across all other cricket pitches while everyone cheered. I think play was held up for five minutes as we all laughed!

I was a kid in an Indian community with a revolution simmering outside, but here in the homes of our cricket opposition's families, there was no disunity, no division, no real difference. There was just kindness, generosity and our shared love of cricket.

Many years later, Nelson Mandela spoke his immortal words about the power of sport to inspire and unite people to break down racial barriers. This sentiment perfectly encapsulates my enlightening experience in the townships as a growing boy.

This is exactly what playing cricket in 'forbidden' townships and my involvement in sport has done for me ever since, energising me to become a part of the positive changes that sport can inspire.

Like so many young white men in South Africa at the time, after school I had a decision to make: be conscripted into two years of obligatory military service or evade it by enrolling at university. I signed up for a Bachelor of Commerce degree at one of South Africa's leading academic institutions, the University of the Witwatersrand ('Wits'), but after battling through the first year I decided to opt for a radical change.

I switched to what I enjoyed most – sport, and a full-time, four-year higher diploma in Physical Education. Being a fully-trained sports and academic teacher was – and is – an important advantage in coaching, as opposed to coaches who just gain a qualification in their specific field.

After completion, I decided to pursue further study, undertaking degrees in History and Philosophy. Apart from my thirst for knowledge, studying was also a way for young white men with a conscience to avoid conscription into the Apartheid juggernaut's dreaded military service. 'Draft-dodging' in those days carried a maximum penalty of six years' imprisonment, but as long as I was studying, I was 'off the hook' and free to explore my great love of sport. I went on to represent my university in cricket, hockey, tennis and table tennis.

After university and while abroad I continued to study, doing a three-year correspondence degree in Psychology only to miss my final examinations due to the birth of my daughter, who arrived on the same day. Nothing was going to keep me from the ecstatic miracle of witnessing that.

My life's pursuit of improvement and knowledge has also brought diplomas in sports psychology, a psychodynamic counselling course, a certificate in sports psychology and five different tennis qualifications.

I love learning languages. I have four (English, Afrikaans, Portuguese and Japanese) under my belt. I worked on Japanese for two years prior to my visit to the 2019 Rugby World Cup. I am a beginner in a couple of others and will convert these to fluency. One of my life's ambitions is to be able to communicate in at least seven languages.

My interest in yoga and meditation has resulted in me taking several relevant courses, retreats and lessons in these spiritual, mental and physical disciplines. Such experiences have provided me with a wealth of knowledge and several interesting and amusing stories.

Once while traveling through Israel, I observed a guy juggling, and this has turned into a personal passion. Although I could already do a basic three-ball juggle, it was the variety and the creativeness he displayed that inspired me. Vicariously, this influenced my creativity in the coaching sphere.

Juggling has proved useful in various ways. It sharpens reflexes, is great for hand-eye coordination and can really put fun into lessons. A few tricks or daring juggles can break the ice in working situations or lessons. Even top golfer Rory McIlroy now uses juggling as part of his preparation routine.

Having avoided the military conscription noose which had been tightening around my neck for nine years of ongoing studies, I eventually decided to flee my homeland. My parents had British ancestry and were keen for me to embrace my heritage, and I am very pleased I did. Britain is an amazing place. It was a daunting prospect to leave home on my own, but with my natural resilience and in-born optimism, I was determined to succeed.

In London, I learned what it is like to be poor and homeless, and discovered the comforts of unknown stairwells, a friend's dingy attic and the bone-numbing floor of a building site in the new Docklands where I found work as a labourer.

It was at this point that my specialising in tennis took off. I had coached part-time in South Africa where I was fortunate to have a floodlit court at our family house. I also ran afternoon clubs as well as tennis and sports camps in the school holidays. Some relatives heard I was slaving away in the Docklands and asked why I wasn't doing something in sport in which they knew I was well qualified, something I was good at as well as enjoyed.

I took a few classes at a North London club on a trial basis as one of their main coaches was away. Without trying to be arrogant, I subsequently heard that people I coached contacted the owners and insisted I coach them in future. The same thing happened after running a holiday camp for them. Most of the kids and parents just wanted me to coach. They were told they had to play with the coach they were given, and so people started arranging lessons in the park and at private houses with me personally. Subsequently, I was able to start my own business.

This was extremely successful until my parents wanted the family to have a base in Europe, which was when we obtained a house with a tennis court in Portugal. I taught at a few clubs there, and my business took off. Again, circumstances brought me back to the UK and once again I built a successful tennis business which has now been running for over 25 years.

It really is thanks to my lasting commitment to sport that my unusual journey has paid off, and I have been fortunate to have watched some of the world's greatest sporting events live – from World Cup finals in football, rugby union and rugby league, to the Olympic Games in 2012, as well as Wimbledon and French Open tennis finals.

The privilege of witnessing hundreds of live, elite matches highlights my passion for experiencing great live sporting events, which in turn has allowed me to analyse first-hand the highest levels of sporting endeavour and achievement.

I've witnessed iconic moments such as Andy Murray winning Wimbledon in 2013, the first British male to achieve the feat since Fred Perry 77 years earlier. It was mesmerising to watch Murray freeze with three championship points on his serve, as the loudest crowd I've ever heard – in over 100 days of watching tennis live at SW19 – roared their encouragement. His opponent, Novak Djokovic, eventually succumbed to the psychological pressure of the British fans.

At the 2006 World Cup football final I saw France legend, Zinedine Zidane, being sent off, having reacted to verbal abuse from Italy defender Marco Materazzi. Zidane's infamous headbutt proved a dramatic farewell to his playing career. I witnessed all this while sitting four rows behind Sir Alex Ferguson and Eric Cantona.

Then there was the incredible 'non-goal' of Frank Lampard in the England v Germany second-round clash at the World Cup in South Africa four years later. By a quirk of fate, my son and I were positioned in line with the 'goal' and clearly saw the ball cross the line after hitting the underside of the crossbar.

I have also watched matches in different sports at all levels, including numerous games as a coach and parent. I have observed with a critical, analytical eye, and through my search for improvement and understanding, have gained new perspectives and insight into the art and science of sport.

While watching sport at any level is interesting, it is witnessing the pinnacle of a game first-hand that helped define and refine RACER. Any good play or mistake can be spotted with the RACER system, giving observers, coaches and players alike a unique and game-changing perspective.

Although I am on the board of the British Tennis Coaches' Association, I haven't looked for national or international acclaim as a coach or writer. Perhaps I have been too content within my immediate environment to spend the time and effort marketing myself and the RACER concept to a wider audience. And yet, I feel the wait has been worth it and that the timing is perfect.

Apart from the unadulterated fun and joy that sport brings me, tennis legend Andre Agassi perhaps best sums up my motives for pursuing my coaching career, and for publishing this book:

> *"Remember this. Hold on to this. This is the only perfection there is, the perfection of helping others. This is the only thing we can do that has any lasting meaning. This is why we're here."*

I am certain everyone can learn something valuable from this book. It offers numerous insights and perspectives, with some great stories and playful anecdotes to open up your understanding of RACER, coaching, playing and watching just about any sport on the planet.

If I can make any difference to people's lives because of this book, it will be an immensely satisfying addition to my life's work and an honour to my enduring passion for the wonderful world of sport. Above all, as Goethe's Clown said at the beginning of this chapter, HAVE FUN and ENJOY!

Mike

Cambridge, UK, *2020*

INTRODUCTION

"The principle is competing against yourself. It's about self-improvement, about being better than you were the day before."
– STEVE YOUNG

Do you want to be the next Lionel Messi, Roger Federer, Jessica Ennis, or Usain Bolt? What about Tiger Woods, Jonnie Peacock, Marta, Lindsey Vonn, or Sachin Tendulkar?

Superstars are one in a million and although I can't guarantee you will attain such heights in your chosen field, with all the wealth, fame, pain and glory that goes with it, I am confident that RACER will dramatically improve and maximise your potential, not only in your sporting discipline, but in many aspects of your involvement and interaction with sport.

The Ultimate Sportsperson

Why is Michael Jordan one of the greatest sports personalities in history? Actually, there are many reasons for this. Some say that his height, strength, speed, power, team ethic, determination, and professionalism have been seen before. That may be true. But most pertinent to this book is that Michael Jordan fulfils, to perfection, each of the five elements that form RACER. As you are about to learn, sport is not an arbitrary collection of actions. Rather, there is a pattern, an underlying system, to the process of sport. If you watch Jordan, you will see him fulfilling the necessary actions each and every time.

I look forward to showing you these five elements. You will see not only in Jordan, but all great sports people, the fulfilment of my RACER principles.

So, what is RACER about?

RACER is an acronym whose five letters outline, in order, the events in time that occur in sport, i.e.:

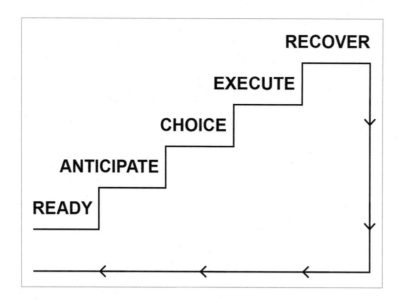

The philosophy behind RACER basically states there is an ordered, specific sequence of essential observations and actions that are required and occur when playing any sport. By understanding and implementing the RACER sequence, your full potential is unlocked, thus sharpening and polishing your:

- Insights
- Understanding
- Thinking
- Performance
- Learning Skills
- Creativity

By understanding the RACER time breakdown, you gain more control of your sporting abilities and environment.

My extensive coaching and observational experience have granted me the confidence to share this ground-breaking RACER system. Although tennis has been my primary coaching sport for the last few decades, the tricks and techniques which I have honed through RACER can be applied to every sport. In fact, when I play any sport, RACER is my personal default point of analysis to get the best out of my performances.

The objective of this book is to give you this new power of knowledge from the RACER system, through a combination of explanation, analysis, examples, stories and assessment charts. Your whole approach and understanding to playing, coaching and watching sport are about to change forever – for the better. For those more concerned with the coaching side of sport, SELF in Chapter 7 presents the four essential foundations to success in the psychology of coaching.

There are some amazing specialist coaches and players, past and present, with incredible knowledge and clever systems of coaching and analysis. But RACER presents a new and unique analysis that will add to your existing knowledge and, in many cases, make a significant difference to any coach, player or observer.

All five elements of the RACER sequence – **Ready, Anticipate, Choice, Execute** and **Recover** – apply to all levels of play in any sporting discipline.

What Is 'RACER'? Whatcha Got?

RACER offers an unparalleled insight into the hidden workings of time in sport. I would like the reader to see sport on this RACER canvas of time, which opens an in-depth understanding of all the multitudinous actions, situations, movements, patterns, positions, variations and excitement in sport.

In almost any sporting discipline, what appear as arbitrary or automatic moments in time and space have a definable pattern, a continuing, evolving, changing pattern that holds the secret to your success. This basic generic sequence lies at the root of all our sporting endeavours. While each sport has its own rules and actions, they all fit into the essential pattern and time sequence that RACER encapsulates.

As in life, there is a flow to sport – a start, a middle and an end. But why break time down? Why show such detail and analysis? What is the big deal? Why is there a book called *RACER* at all? The big deal is that KNOWLEDGE IS POWER. The big deal is that understanding RACER can make the difference between personal or team mediocrity, and personal or team excellence. That's Whatcha Got…

I Spy With My Little Eye…

When complexity, variations, deviations and the unexpected are all considered in any sport, we are left with essential sequences, i.e., the RACER pattern.

A series of mental and physical occurrences that, if you were to freeze frame them from beginning to end would, by a quirk of good luck and convenience, constitute the acronym RACER.

Ready **A**nticipate **C**hoice **E**xecute **R**ecover

1. Everything starts with being **Ready** - mentally, tactically and physically Ready for the action about to take place.
2. Next is to try and **Anticipate** what your opponents' or team-mates' next action might be and react as soon as possible.
3. Once you know the outcome of their actions, you make a **Choice** as to what is the best action to take.
4. You now need to **Execute** your Choice, using both your mental and physical abilities.
5. Finally, once you have Executed, you **Recover,** Review or, as some of my wise-cracking pupils suggest, 'Regret'!

Then, instantly or naturally we return to Ready, and the cycle continues.

RACER – What Can It Do For You?

RACER offers a different, more informative and pragmatic perspective on sport than most people would have come across. Just as importantly, whether with pupils, associates or friends on social media, or anywhere you interact in relation to sport, you will possess new insights with which to express thoughts and ideas.

A crucial benefit or advantage of RACER is that it allows pupils to analyse, evaluate and understand their own game. This instils self-awareness, confidence, and independence from outside sources, resulting in a freedom and responsibility to achieve improved performances. There is a current trend in sport, from the coaching to playing arenas, to get players to take responsibility, to make decisions, to think, understand and act.

Coaches can plan far more pragmatic sessions. Because RACER looks at the play in sequence, it helps access causes, not effects. Coaches can thus plan and set up with more appropriate, relevant exercises, drills and workouts than just routine sessions. Not only as above, but within sessions, the ability to access causes not effects means better feedback and working suggestions. Thus a 'bad' pass may be due to the receiver not Anticipating the pass.

In addition, if pundits understood this conceptual approach, we would be getting a far more perceptive and informed commentary as our preferred sporting action unfolds. Too often, we are left in the dark by facile and superficial scrutiny from commentators and analysts. Often, they add zero value and I listen and wish I could show them how to use the RACER system and the value to the quality of their work that RACER would add.

My first aim is for people to understand the basic system. This will be followed by explaining RACER overlaps and inter-relations, as the dynamics of sport do not exclusively occur in the linear sequence I initially suggest. There are vital combinations within RACER, and one option explains how you can start learning, teaching or improving from any point within the RACER sequence.

This added, more complex information later in the book will further enhance your knowledge, thus allowing you deeper perspectives and more alternatives for coaching practise and matchplay.

I will not be able to delve into every nuance and detail as there are aspects within each area of RACER that require further specialisation and space. An example is eye coaching, in which notable advancements have been made this century. There are very specialised and specific details to this, yet the point at a basic-to-advanced level is better use of our visual system. Thus, in Anticipation, looking at the correct cues or movements of your opponents, you will obtain earlier, more enlightening information and you can thus make better Choices.

Once I had the knowledge from RACER, my confidence and belief in my coaching and my individual performance soared. Money makes money but likewise, knowledge makes more knowledge. My awareness increased as I sought ways to teach these new skills. From a coaching perspective (in this instance, mainly though not exclusively tennis), not only had I now introduced new and exciting ideas and analysis, but I was also now looking at causes, not symptoms.

For example, why does someone keep hitting the ball too high or too far when they have been told many times to focus on closing the face of the racket to keep the ball down? The answer is that they didn't realise the ball was lifting faster and higher than Anticipated. Therefore, they would hit under the ball, causing it to go too high in the air.

In this case, correcting the Execution was not dealing with the cause of the bad Execution. The problem was not the symptom of the open racket face. The pupil had to Anticipate the rising ball, and this addressed a major reason *behind* the error in Execution. Thus, the key to improved performance lay in correcting the 'why', not the 'how', i.e., Anticipation.

Another example: when seeing someone make a silly mistake, the focus is usually to look at the Execution. But perhaps the player was running out of puff and chose to make that risky Execution out of desperation or lack of thinking, such as someone shooting wildly at goal, or a shot in a racket or bat sport. RACER gives an understanding of the reasons behind the Choices we make.

Sometimes comments are made, such as, "You are too slow", or "You let your opponent get away from you." But these are symptoms, not causes. The actual cause was that the person perhaps didn't Recover or wasn't in a good Ready position, and this was why the error occurred.

Such analysis catalysed tremendous improvements in my pupils' individual abilities, but then to my initial surprise I realised it works equally well in pairs or team sports. At the time, this was an incredibly exciting revelation to me, i.e., all sports work off the same generic system.

However, as obvious or simple as RACER appears, I have consistently seen – at all levels of sports performance and coaching – that this sequence is not fully understood and followed. Some examples include:

- Players not being Ready, their mind still on their previous action or displaying a lack of focus.
- Coaches expecting players to make a Choice when they have little or no idea of Anticipation.
- Wrong Choices being made in matches and coaching, with subsequent difficult Execution.
- Poor Execution for several reasons including technical or mental, with often too little emphasis or understanding placed on the psychological/mental aspect of Execution.
- Finally, instead of Recovering, players watch the Execution, or they don't Recover enough – tactically or physically.

By getting to know the RACER system, players will learn to understand more about their approach to their sport and can take greater responsibility for their actions.

The Evolution of the Acronym 'RACER'

Some years ago, I was in a very difficult coaching situation struggling to find a solution to help a pupil improve…

I had been coaching a tennis student for two years (yes, he owned a very successful fish and chips company!) but his progress had started to plateau. His technique was excellent, besides the odd reminder, but his improvement in lessons was slowing and our connection was slipping. In addition, his recent match results had not been as positive as we had wanted.

I was becoming frustrated and concerned, having worked exceptionally hard with him through this tough period. I take my role personally, so this was hurting me.

I then decided to watch him during a match and visualised what I would be choosing, and where I would be moving. What was very noticeable were the images not matching. His Choices weren't mine; his movement wasn't mine.

For example, he would be on the back foot behind the baseline and hit a low shot into the net, when the better percentage Choice would have been to hit a high shot down the middle.

On the return of a first serve, the highest percentage shot is to go back at the server. However, my student was trying to hit too many shots cross-court or down the line, for winners. A few worked, but he often either missed or was giving his opponent time to get to the ball and hit a decent shot.

So, I needed to work on his Choice, and this became the focus over the next few lessons - firstly working on the comments above, but also on his Choice of serve. The emphasis was on developing an awareness of Choice and the variety of best possible Choices at his disposal. We worked on his Choice in game situations during lessons and it was clear that there was dramatic improvement. The next match he played produced significant improvement in his Choices, which was very satisfying and interesting to watch. His play had improved purely through making better Choices.

But I still wasn't completely satisfied, because I also noted some occasions where the correct Choice did not occur. When we discussed this post-match, focusing on a few specific situations and shots that had occurred, it was apparent that his Anticipation was not as developed as it could have been. Thus, his Choice of shot was affected by poor Anticipation.

For example, while I noted his opponent using heavy slice (backspin) without much power, thus a defensive shot, my Choice would have been to advance, take the floating ball in the air and put away the volley, or take the ball early and attack. But because of poor Anticipation, his Choice was limited (defensive), thus losing an opportunity to put pressure on his opponent.

Our next lessons thus focused on Anticipating and Choosing. This got me thinking that there could be a consistent sequence to follow in real time. This could help improve a person's play because the player would follow and know what was required in the correct sequence, i.e., first Anticipate then Choice.

Then it struck me: after you Choose your shot, you must Execute it, not in the obvious sense of hitting the ball but because of a specific Choice. My mind was now in full swing, and I was aware something unique was afoot.

Now I had the acronym ACE: Anticipate – Choice – Execute.

From a coaching point of view, there was a sound working formula in place. I could trace good and bad shots and point to the successful application of these three phases of play. In retrospect, what comes first in the sequence seems obvious. But at the time, I didn't immediately see it and had to keep thinking, "What's next?" and "Is there more?". Aware of a sequence occurring, surely there was more than ACE.

Soon after, I was coaching a pupil on a lovely British summer day.

As he warmed up, I said: "Make sure you are Ready today as we are really going to ACE this lesson." I then shouted out "yes, yes!", to the bemusement of my pupil. I realised and explained that the first part of the acronym was the 'R' for Ready. RACE had arrived.

So, I now had RACE. That sounded easy to remember, as well as practical – my pupils had to RACE. I really plugged this concept with positive results. There was a sense of a genuine discovery, something special. I felt like a scientist discovering a secret code.

Again, looking back, it might appear obvious, but although I was so busy basking in my joy of RACE, at some point I realised I hadn't quite finished. Perhaps, subconsciously, I felt people weren't getting Ready as well as they should have done.

The reason for not ideal Readiness was that they were not Recovering as well or appropriately as they should have been. So, there I had it: put Recovery after the Execution and I had the full code. An acronym that sounded good, and had depth, and was easy to apply and remember. Now that really sounded complete: RACER. With a smile on my face, I greeted many a class, telling them I had found the missing link.

"You shouldn't have looked in the mirror," came one teasing remark. Other suggestions when I told people I had found the last letter and that it started with 'R' included rejoice, retry, regret and, eventually, some got it – Recover.

So, with great joy and enthusiasm I began the long, informative and formative exploration of RACER. The one notable and interesting point was that RACER immediately started to help me improve my game. And from a coaching perspective, it changed everything for me.

Retrospectively, each step of RACER seemed obvious, but at the time I had to weed each element out, step by step, day by day, week by week, thought by thought. I saw pupils developing with the system, getting a better understanding and improvement in their own performance as I worked towards the final, complete RACER concept.

RACER is not dogmatic or inflexible: it is experimental, malleable, open to epistemological enquiry. While the core of the RACER sequence remains stable and strong, each person can use and teach it however they wish. The point is there is vast room for personal application and implementation. Each person using their understanding of RACER needs to experience first-hand the practical implications.

Only the effectiveness of a system can test its veracity. Does it help? Does it work for you? Can you find better ways to play, train, teach and watch, while using RACER principles? My answer is a resounding YES.

The RACER system was born out of my striving, cumulative experiences and desire to achieve something special, as well as an enduring passion for being the best for my pupils, something which my Southern Hemisphere background has instilled in me.

A childhood memory recalls seeing nothing other than a collection of plastic rackets, balls and sports objects floating dreamily above my cot in what can only be described as the most indoctrinating 'mobile' in the world. From the word go, I don't think I had much Choice other than to be a lifelong sports fanatic.

This book is the result of insights which my mind was subconsciously searching for, i.e. a brilliant coaching system. RACER is the result of the accumulation, distillation and delineation of all my acquired knowledge from decades of studying, coaching and watching sport. It offers the condensed experience of my devotion and expertise as a coach and a player. I believe you, too, will benefit from understanding and applying the RACER system in whatever capacity you use it.

Read on – your game is waiting to step up to the next level!

Chapter 1

READY

"The readiness is all"
- WILLIAM SHAKESPEARE, *HAMLET*

One of the keys to our enjoyment and success, in any sport we play or coach, is the fascinating and much-undervalued skill of being dynamically Ready, both before and during every appropriate moment of the game. Understanding this when watching sport also enhances analysis generally and specifically at critical moments. Some may say Ready is obvious, yet week in and week out I see world-class professionals failing to make the grade on this aspect. Being Ready is not an obvious state to be in - it needs work and attention.

Incidents in both NFL football and rugby union highlight the importance of being Ready in general as well as being Ready as a team. This is especially true when you are close to winning.

The Blood Brothers Final and Lights Go Out

The 48th Super Bowl played in New Orleans was an incredible match between the Baltimore Ravens and the San Francisco 49ers for several reasons. Firstly, for the first time in Super Bowl history, two brothers, John and Jim Harbaugh, were the opposing head coaches. It was also the first time both teams were undefeated in previous Super Bowls. And finally, the lights went out at half time for forty minutes, with the Ravens leading 28-6! The Ravens lost their momentum, conceding 17 points without reply. The game came down to the final drive, but the Ravens held on to win.

The Greatest Comeback Defeat in the History of Sport

In a similar vein, the England rugby union team were 31-0 up at home to Scotland in the Six Nations with 30 minutes on the clock. They then conceded an unprecedented 38 points and scored a last gasp try, converted in front of the posts to avoid the greatest comeback defeat in the sport's history at the top level.

Both matches are examples of the teams in the lead losing their focus and not being Ready. This invariably affects their performance, and gives the opposition a window of opportunity to fight back.

On the positive side, I'd like you to consider for a moment how truly unforgettable goals, those knife-edge victories and jaw-dropping, last-second winners that make sport so thrilling, actually come to pass (if you'll excuse the pun). How was that stunning victory humanly possible and where did the magic come from in those final, nail-biting moments?

Cynics might explain some unbelievable wins as being unearned, saying, 'The match was given away' or 'What a fluke'. They might put it down to luck. Sure, 'pure luck' exists, but winners make their own good fortune, and it starts with being Ready. The perennial high performers have found their mark by paying perfect attention to being dynamically Ready throughout the game.

Understanding the first phase of the RACER sequence – Ready – will help you see that those split-second, winning reactions, at any level in any game, are in fact well-honed, constant, and highly informed actions that have been developed through rigorous practice and minute attention to detail.

When I discuss Ready, many people say to me "yeah, yeah, yeah" but, in fact, as already noted, dynamic Readiness is not done as well as it should be and there is more depth and skill than most people realise. I will elaborate in this chapter.

Brought Back Down To Earth

In early 2019, I hit one of most amazing shots for a long time in an exhibition doubles match at my academy. The ball was wide of my backhand, I lunged out, acutely angling my racket, grip loosened for control, my dynamic balance tested. The ball, with just the right pace and angle, proved too good for my opponents. Quite a few people were watching, and I yelled with delight as the applause and whooping rang out. Then I heard my son's exasperated-yet-firm didactic voice: "Dad, why the hell are you standing there?"

After the initial shock to myself and the spectators, I realised he was right. I was totally out of position and was forced to play that great shot.

Being Ready is very closely linked with Recovery. You can't be Ready if you don't Recover. But, in fact, your Recovery will also be more difficult if you aren't Ready, as you could possibly play a more difficult shot, and it becomes a vicious cycle.

Are you Ready to be RACER Ready?

Any efficient and effective process requires motivation, preparation, action and determination.

> *To be RACER Ready is to be in a state of Physical, Tactical, Technical and Psychological (PTTP) preparedness. To be dynamically Ready is to perform at optimum PTTP Readiness.*

The Four-Factor RACER Ready Essentials

Here is a short summary of the four key aspects:

- Physical – Here, a combination of as many bodily skills as possible is required. This includes agility, balance, coordination, speed, power, endurance, sight, hearing and strength.
- Tactical – Where is the best place to be Ready? There is little use in jumping around in a physical Ready posture if you are in the wrong place. So being in the right tactical position at the right time is essential.
- Technical – The way you use your body, or the biomechanics to achieve a specific task is important. How to jump at the right height and timing to get into the Ready position, for example. Or the way you pivot to turn the body, leading with the head to give the best physical chance of success.
- Psychological – A state of mental equilibrium and emotional strength to maintain a focused mind, whatever the situation, be you under the cosh, outclassing your opponents, or in a tight and tense game.

So, while the four can be practiced in isolation, the aim is combining them in the best way for yourself or the team to help perform at the optimum level. Whether you're a beginner just wanting to improve, a talented amateur or an aspiring champion, the core principles of being Ready remain the same.

Whatever your relationship to sport, you need to be aware of – and improve – on the Ready position in all its dimensions. The difference in the *quality* of our Ready state is a key factor that determines our performance and, crucially, our enjoyment levels.

Understanding your state and the importance of being Ready is often the secret to winning or losing in sport; the difference between really *enjoying* your game or just playing around and becoming frustrated.

Ready Scenarios

There are many situations, aspects and complexities related to being Ready. Below is a breakdown of some very important ones

- Pre-match routines
- The pre-match bubble
- The start of each sequence during action
- After each action and phase of play
- Breaks such as half-time or changeover

Me, You, Everybody

This refers to the three different permutations of Ready:

1. Individual Readiness

In this case, being Ready is up to you. You take full responsibility for being or coaching dynamically Ready. You know the four factors. Work on them, perform them.

2. Partner Readiness

This requires you working and being aware of your partner – and they of you. In this scenario, the tactical situation would be prominent, as working in unison and understanding is vital to get you both in the best possible position. Thus, if your partner is attacking you should be in the best position to support them. The same applies with defence, to be in the best position from which you can transition to neutral or give the opponents the most difficult Ready tactical play to hurt you.

The mental factor of being there and supporting each other is also vital to the quality of your Ready state of mind. This means knowing each other and getting the other person to be in the best mental state possible. This could be done verbally or even with a good tap on the back.

We also, of course, need to be aware of our own personal Readiness responsibilities, i.e., physical and technical performance.

3. Team Readiness

In teams, Ready has many more variables. Firstly, you perform all your essential Readiness factors. Secondly, perform in pairs or groups. For example, how the goalkeeper gets Ready with the defence in mind, and vice versa. How the midfielder works with the striker. In cricket, how bowlers work as units together, or the wicketkeeper with the bowler. In effect, mini units within a team. Thirdly, perform as a group. For example, how does the team keep its shape? This requires everyone getting into their Ready position and recovering to the 'Team Position'.

So, a combination of individual, working with a team-mate, and collective responsibility is required: a collective and interchangeable responsibility which varies for different scenarios. This includes situations of defence, neutral and attack in the fluidity of the game, as well as the very important set pieces, such as a hit or throw-in, corners, free-kicks, penalties, etcetera.

As with partners, the tactical and mental factors are prominent collectively. By being efficient, your individual physical and technical Ready factors will be in a far better state for you to be able to perform team Ready requirements.

Staying in the flow or the zone, because we constantly need to be Ready for the next phase or action, is discussed with authority in the 1999 book *Flow in Sports* by Susan A. Jackson and Mihaly Csikszentmihalyi. Ready is about the ability to keep the right mindset to act. Thus, there are different levels of intensity of Ready. The ball may be on the far side and you may not need to be immediately called into action, and yet you need a level of Readiness that means if you were called into action, you would be dynamically Ready to respond.

A great example of awareness of being Ready can be seen in the following story:

Are You *Ready* or Are You Ready?

A confident squash pupil of mine came to my coaching session one day and, despite my protestations, insisted he was mostly in the correct Ready position at the start and during a point. So, I came up with an idea. He was to shout "ready" whenever he was in position and Ready.

It soon became apparent that he was not nearly as proficient at being Ready as he had presumed, as often I hit the ball before he had a chance to say, "ready". He gave me that great look of acknowledgement and we worked hard on improving.

He proudly finished the lesson with a near faultless 'ready shouting' performance and, on the last point, a pointedly clear "ready" was shouted, with him making no attempt to hit the ball, followed by a withering stare in my direction and the utterance of "happy?". I'm pleased to say the session ended in a great laugh for both of us. I subsequently tried this on a tennis court, and it's a great way to get pupils or players to Recover and be Ready.

American football is a sport which - if you know nothing about it - often appears to be a game with a bit of action followed by incessant breaks in play. But once you understand the sport, you realise that the time with the ball in play is so intense that it's thrilling to watch. Because the time with the ball in play is so short, one vital element is needed without fail.

This element is being Ready. Watch the low stance of the forwards of both teams. Mentally and physically, they are Ready for the most intense and dynamic movement in sport. Their movements are not at great angles, but rather pure forward or slightly off centre movements. The outside players are not so low, because their movement is often forward and lateral. They are still intensely Ready. They are not as low for power, but rather for speed and flexibility of direction.

The 'Five-Minute Final'

Even at the highest levels of football, you can spot which players are and aren't in a constant state of being dynamically Ready. Of course, the higher the level the more dynamically Ready players must be, but even the best let it slip.

The 1979 FA Cup final between Arsenal and Manchester United saw the Red Devils hit back from two-down to level, with goals in the 86th and 88th minutes. Still celebrating the equaliser and having maybe underestimated the character of a stunned Arsenal side, United dropped their guard and the Londoners immediately raced up the other end. As an ardent United fan, the heart-stopper came when Alan Sunderland nipped in to score what proved to be the 89th-minute winner.

The match has since become known as the 'Five-Minute Final' and it always reminds me how easy it is to take being Ready for granted, even when you think the game is in the bag or you have done enough. From a RACER perspective I look at the PTTP, to assess what was happening. In the end United, having done the hard work, let the game slip due to the failure of their team dynamic Ready position. Their minds drifted in the wake of their astonishing initial comeback.

Physically Ready

The more physically Ready you are, the more able you are to efficiently respond to the next action. The first change I make when a pupil starts improving, or if my opponent plays at a strong level, is in my physical Ready position. An observer could note the level of my pupil or opponent by watching my Ready position.

Preparing to be physically Ready requires varying amounts of training and effort. Some of the essential basics of being physically Ready for all aspects of sport include the following:

- Agility
- Balance
- Coordination
- Speed and strength
- Reflexes and reactions
- Eye control
- Flexibility and suppleness
- Endurance, including cardiovascular and respiratory endurance
- Special attention to specific muscle groupings

Body language and physical presence add to the physically Ready mix. Tennis legend Serena Williams is known to exude such an air of confidence and physical dominance that she is literally scary to some opponents.

During net training, I often tell my pupils to be large like a giant who can get to anything and has no fear, rather than the antithesis, making themselves small and praying the ball comes nowhere near them.

The better the quality of all these physically Ready components, the more productive and effective your dynamically READY position will be. As the saying goes:

"By failing to prepare you are preparing to fail."

Eye Ready, One of the Modern Advances in Sports Science

I often stress the importance of eye Readiness. If you are just staring hopefully into the distance, without a specific eye purpose or intensive focus, if you're not constantly 'on the lookout' then you are not eye Ready.

Great players consciously maximise the use of their eyes with the help of specialist coaches like Dr Sherylle Calder.

Dr Calder sat on the bench for England's victorious rugby union World Cup campaign in 2003 and for the next tournament four years later with the victorious South Africa squad. Both winning coaches, Sir Clive Woodward and Jake White, recognised the indispensable importance of how players use their eyes and visual training to maximise performance.

It's important to remember the difference in eye Readiness between individual and team or pairs sports. For instance, in individual racket sports the eyes have a highly specific focus as you concentrate on the

Anticipation of your opponent's racket, bat or body movement. While peripheral vision is used, it's not as important as in team sports where your awareness of your team and opponents is vital to performing well.

Body Language Baggage

"Enthusiasm is everything. It must be taut and vibrating like a string"

– PELÉ

While coaching a hockey team in a practice match, my players found themselves 3-0 down. After we conceded the third goal, I looked around and made eye contact with various players, asking them if they were Ready. They all forlornly nodded. At that point I stopped the game, and called them in.

"Boys," I said, "you are not Ready. Most of you are only partially physically Ready, but your body language shows me you could be looking far more positive than you are. And this means you are not *really* Ready.

"Your posture generally reflects your state of mind. You are carrying baggage that you need to get rid of," I continued. "If someone were to walk past right now, they could tell that you guys had just conceded a goal from noticing your body language instead of thinking you had just scored. So, think of your next great pass, think of scoring a goal.

"Now get back out there, put your shoulders back and look hungry, look up for it. Get on your toes, show some enthusiasm, encourage each other, and let's go!"

After the break, their performance picked up so remarkably that the other coach came up to me after the game and remarked: "Goodness me, what on earth did you say to them? They were transformed."

Positive body language and showing enthusiasm, even when you're down, is an integral part of being physically Ready.

Technically Ready

Related to the physical side of Ready, technical Readiness is also specific to the situation you find yourself in. Are you at the start of a sequence? Have you just recovered? What is the tactical plan? What are you anticipating?

What follows is an overview of some of the factors that can affect your technical movements, usually referring to specific tasks:

- How wide is your Ready stance?
- How bent should your knees be?
- How high is your Ready jump?
- Which foot is in front?
- How do you pivot?
- How do you shift your weight?
- How do you move to the next position?

The aim is for efficiency of movement. The correct way to turn or pivot and push off, and how low you stay before reaching your natural running height for maximum pace, are two more aspects affecting our technical efficiency. The drop step, small or large first steps. These are all important points that specialist coaches in specific sports and situations concentrate on.

The following anecdotes are good examples of the depth top performers go to, to achieve technical Readiness.

A Matter of Millimetres

I recall a conversation with Jez Green, the ex-physical trainer to British tennis legend Andy Murray and former Wimbledon finalist Tomas Berdych, who now works with top-ten player Alexander Zverev. Green revealed that the Murray team were concentrating on the right height of Murray's jump for the split step. He discussed with me the height of the split step in various situations and positions on the court.

His overriding concern in this particular regard was whether the height after pushing off was too high. I was enthralled by the technical detail and specificity involved, the attention to minute detail. Anything to improve his game, if only by a fractionally small margin – maybe the difference between a Grand Slam or not?

Before Bolt Bolts

The area of technical Readiness was one of the major aspects of being dynamically Ready for the world's greatest-ever sprint athlete, Usain Bolt.

It is well known that as a perceived slow starter, the Jamaican spent many hours working on the technical aspects of his start. My son and I were fortunate to be only 20 metres from him at the start of his victorious 200m run at the London 2012 Olympic Games, with a prime view of where the great man warmed up.

We intently watched not only how he prepared mentally and physically, but the way he was working on and practicing his technique for the start of the race.

Some aspects which the 'Lightning' Bolt's mind might have been focusing on are:

- How low to keep his head down until reaching full extension
- How soon to reach for full stride length, remembering that if you do this too early you take longer to get to maximum pace

Bolt's preparation illustrates that, while people may think that the start of a race is not as important as many other aspects, in fact, being in the correct Ready position and frame of mind is essential to success.

Tactical Readiness

Tactical positioning is a vital weapon. You may be super prepared physically and mentally, but if you are in the wrong area, you could pay the price. While each sport has its tactical possibilities, there are also common grounds and principles that apply in relation to the tactical Readiness in all sports. The following examples will illustrate the importance of tactical Readiness:

Example 1 – In football, it is essential for the defensive unit to move up as a group to try and catch the attacking team offside. Yes, one loner, through a lack of concentration or laziness can scupper this objective with the possibility of conceding a vital goal. This tactical awareness and efficiency is vital to a successful defensive unit.

An example of tactical Readiness, not forgetting the link of Readiness with Recovery, took place in the 2018 Champions League semi-final. Having lost 3-0 at home in the first leg, Juventus stunned Real Madrid in the return to draw level on aggregate in front of over 75,000 raucous home spectators.

No side had ever come back from such a home loss to win an away tie. Then, disaster struck for Juve when English referee Michael Oliver awarded a 90th-minute penalty to Real for an apparent push in the area. Furious with the referee, their players and supporters – and subsequently the Italian press – went berserk, with goalkeeper Gianluigi Buffon being sent off for protesting the decision. The spot-kick was eventually converted by Cristiano Ronaldo seven minutes after the award! From a RACER point of view, this is not the issue.

My point is not about the penalty decision, but concerns the very poor tactical Ready position of the Juventus player, Medhi Benatia, giving away the spot-kick. He should have been closer to the attacker, Lucas Vazquez, perhaps even on the other side of him, but he was watching and not recovering into the optimum tactical Ready position. Hewas thus forced to make a dangerous and unnecessary challenge because of this failure.

Example 2 – The 2017 third Ashes Test in Perth saw the English side already two-down in the five-match series against Australia, fighting for survival in what is considered cricket's most famous, historic rivalry.

After two dropped catches in the England slip cordon, the commentators wondered if the tactical position of the slip fielders was correct. Some suggested that two players were too close, while others ruminated that the staggered formation perhaps wasn't a good idea due to the conditions.

Whatever the real problem was, it was clear that England were throwing chances away due to poor tactical fielding positions.

Example 3 – Deciding where you stand to serve or receive serve in racket sports is a well-known tactic. In his bid to win a 16th Major title at the 2017 US Open against Kevin Anderson, the massive-serving South African, Rafael Nadal kept changing his Ready position to return serve. At times he stood close to the baseline and at others he stood far back. At one point he even came in closer for the first serve and stood back on the second serve, which is both counter-intuitive and unusual due to the faster pace of the first serve, disturbing Anderson's rhythm and confidence.

Nadal's intelligent unsettling of his opponent and astute tactical Ready positioning was absorbing to watch and helped secure his victory.

Clever tactical positioning can unsettle the most challenging of opponents.

Example 4 – In rugby union, tactical Readiness was aptly illustrated during the first Test of the 2017 British & Irish Lions' tour, a 30-15 defeat by world champions, New Zealand, at Eden Park, Auckland.

After a big kick from the All Blacks was thumped into the Lions' half, one of the Kiwi forwards went steaming up the field and blocked off any attempt at a quick throw-in after it made touch: excellent tactical Readiness.

A while later, a Lion was bundled out of play, giving New Zealand the lineout. The New Zealander grabbed at the ball which was still in the Lions' hands. Instead of the latter throwing the ball away, he unthinkingly handed the ball to his opponent, the opposite of what had occurred earlier. So, a quick lineout was taken.

Less than a minute later, New Zealand scored a try. Put simply, the Lions player should not have allowed the All Blacks to be Ready to restart so swiftly. Taking a lineout quickly before the other team is Ready can be a huge tactical benefit.

The stark difference in awareness of Readiness between the teams drove home the point that tactical Readiness means constant awareness and concentration at the appropriate moments.

Tactical Readiness Possibilities:

- Attack – If you or your team are on the attack, assess exactly what your best tactically Ready positioning is to enhance that attack.
- Neutral – Ready to transition into defence or attack, waiting for the right moment to make the correct decision.
- Defence – To assess the best defensive position requires a degree of foresight and an awareness of the opponent's attacking tactics, as well a knowledge of your teammates.

In all three approaches there is a range within each possibility.

Thus, you can attack with a high risk or low risk of success. You can defend cautiously or safely or be on the defensive but not under extreme threat, thus your Readiness position will be reflected accordingly.

Psychologically Ready

"All things are ready, if our mind be so."
– WILLIAM SHAKESPEARE, *HENRY V*

The final, essential part of being dynamically Ready is the psychological dimension. Simply looking the part and being in the right position at the right time is not enough. If you are psychologically Ready, your physical Readiness is far more likely to succeed.

Sports psychology is a complex science and being psychologically Ready is not simply a case of being overconfident or taking up a positive-only attitude, which is sometimes advocated by coaches.

What is Your Optimum Ready State of Mind?

Being psychologically Ready includes being focused on the action ahead, with the right amount of mental tension leaning more towards a calm rather than an over-excited state of mind. To achieve this state consistently through training or a match is the aim. Remember that levels of focus do fluctuate depending on the intensity and the context within play, e.g., if the ball is off the pitch, the mind is not as intense as when in play.

Finding ways to keep the mind ideally Ready include visualising yourself as Ready, a feeling of 'pounceabilty', i.e., prepared to pounce. Concentration, discipline and determination are further assets in achieving a consistent Readiness.

A few basics, and a few curveball examples here, aim to show that with the right psychological frame of mind, you can achieve remarkable results.

Believing Isn't Everything

Self-confidence is important in any sport, but it's not always just about the belief that you will win or knowing that you're a great player.

When Thomas Johansson returned from injury short of match fitness and won the 2002 Australian Open, he later commented that he had not believed he ever had a chance of winning the tournament. The Swedish tennis star had never progressed beyond a Grand Slam quarter-final before then, and this was his only major success.

Johansson simply went into the competition with no expectations. In a way, he had the psychological mindset that we all try to create. His Ready position psychologically was of no pressure, just the joy of competing. We saw how both the England football team and Andy Murray struggled with the pressure and expectations from the public. It was only when both got themselves Ready to perform at their best, with the right frame of mind, that success was achieved. The problem is how to reach and maintain that state when high hopes, expectations and responsibilities are baying to be satisfied.

A Danish Treat

Another example of the importance of a relaxed mental state is the experience of the Danish football team that failed to qualify for the European Championships in 1992. A little over a week before the tournament, Yugoslavia were banned from competing due to the atrocities and civil war in that country, so as runners-up in their qualifying group, the Danes now took their place.

Many of the players were already enjoying their holidays, including star man Michael Laudrup. Despite this, incredibly, the Danes went on to win the tournament. In fact, several years ago, I was walking through Copenhagen and walking towards me was Laudrup himself! My eyes bulged, and I just blurted out, "1992!". In response he gave a very big smile, and a shake of the head.

Again, having no expectations with nothing to lose, and being happy just to be at the tournament, made for great bonding amongst the players. The Danish players were in an ideal physical and psychological Readiness state to perform to the best of their ability.

> *Being in the right state of mental Readiness, as tiredness and pressure build, is a vitally important skill. How we achieve it best is largely up to us as individuals and coaches, but team building and being relaxed are important to being psychologically Ready.*

Gazzamania – How not to be Dynamically Ready

Paul Gascoigne is one of the most precocious talents ever seen in British football. In the 1991 FA Cup Final against Brian Clough's Nottingham Forest, his last match for Tottenham Hotspurs before a proposed big-money move to the Italian side Lazio, I was at the Wembley match and witnessed Gazza warm up. At the time, I noted to a friend that he looked physiologically and physically out of control. He looked over-enthusiastic and frantic.

The final began with Gazza chasing around like a man possessed.

His second serious foul after 16 minutes on Gary Charles was not only wild and dangerous but led to Forest's goal from Stuart Pearce's free-kick. To make it worse, Gascoigne was forced to come off injured from the same incident.

Gazza himself was aware of this behaviour and Will Magee, writing for *VICE Sports* in May 2016, noted:

> *"He was already renowned for his erratic behaviour... a fizzing firecracker, a ball of nervous energy at all times. He suffered from intense insomnia, such was his excitement before big matches. He claimed to have taken medication the night before the final in a last-ditch effort to control it."*

The point of the story is to illustrate that however talented, enthusiastic and determined you are, without the balance and control of your physical, psychological and personal environment, you will not be dynamically Ready.

Preparing to be Ready

A vital part of becoming dynamically Ready is obviously the mental and physical work of pre-game preparation and training. Observations by two sporting greats illustrate that our best physical, tactical and mental state of being Ready goes way beyond the actual match or game itself:

- On an individual basis, British Olympic 100m breaststroke champion Adam Peaty once spoke about the tiny margins at the elite level. Essentially, just one day missed in training could drop his performance by 0.01 of a second, possibly the difference between a gold or a silver medal.

- On a team level, former England cricket captain Michael Vaughan once commented on a lack of preparation training in some team members during the Ashes series of 2017/18. He was talking about off-the-field negativity after the English had been thoroughly thrashed.

We're not all pros, but the principles remain the same. Before anything in life, a little extra preparation can go a long way towards achieving your own state of dynamic Readiness.

A Crucial Link

I must reinforce the importance of the relationship between psychological Readiness and Recovery.

You can only be psychologically Ready if you have fully and correctly Recovered from the previous phase of action. At the start of the action, one has different types of challenges and interference in terms of being in the best psychological state. By this I mean instances such as the pressure of the match, tiredness, doubt, or the mind still being focused on the previous point, or the last good or bad shot. But during and after points or phases of play, our Recovery is what determines the quality of our psychologically Ready state.

In Summary

Peyton Manning, one of the greats of American football, said:

> *"I never left the field saying I could have done more to get ready and that gives me peace of mind."*

The following is a prime example of how all four PTTPs of Ready combined to deliver remarkable rewards:

Chang Makes A Bang

One of the most remarkable men's Grand Slam successes in history came from unseeded American Michael Chang when he won the 1989 French Open.

In the fourth round that year he faced World No.1 and three-time champion Ivan Lendl, and their match-up is believed by many to be one of the greatest matches in the tournament's history.

There are numerous points of interest from Chang's victory, including an underarm serve as mental and physical fatigue almost forced him to quit. But in this instance, we will concentrate on how the 17-year-old Chang used PTTP to finally outsmart his opponent in the five-set thriller.

At 15-40 down, Lendl served to Chang who was 5-3 up in the final set. In an unbelievable move, Chang walked right up to the service line to receive, completely unsettling Lendl mentally who double faulted, gifting the game, set and match.

Chang realised that physically and technically, because of his cramp, his best Ready position was right up on the service line, which is very rarely ever done. Tactically and psychologically this was also his best move as he would rather rely on reflex to get the ball back at short range, rather than give Lendl more time and force himself to make extra movements from further back in the court. Besides which, this all-round dynamic Ready move totally rattled and frustrated the Czech – who thus lost his own rhythm and dynamic Readiness and consequently, at this vital stage, effectively conceded the match to the American.

A knowledgeable sports coach once said to me, "Yes, amazing, Mike, I like RACER, I like it all, but it's really about being Ready." By being aware of the importance of the Ready position and its dynamic fluidity, and working on all aspects of your physical, technical, tactical and psychological Readiness, you or your team will be able to maximise your start, whether at the literal start of any game, or in the constant, dynamic starts throughout the game.

While on the one hand being Ready seems a very simple and obvious aspect of sport, it is in fact highly complex and vitally important. Breaking Ready down into the physical, technical, tactical and psychological (PTTP) components is a sure way to help gain more insight.

"Winning is the science of being totally prepared."

The above quote comes from the famous American football coach, George Allen. Like any science, being dynamically or athletically Ready involves attending to the tiniest details and constantly refining and improving our bodies, minds and tactics towards an ultimately dynamic state of Readiness.

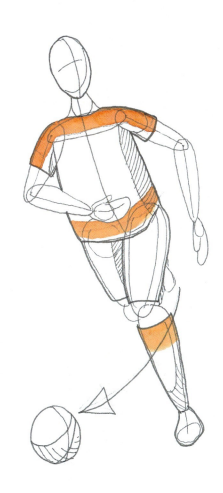

Chapter 2

ANTICIPATION

"Forewarned, forearmed; to be prepared is half the victory."
– Miguel de Cervantes

Anticipation is the ability to use cognitive and intuitive knowledge to predict what is likely to occur next or in the foreseeable future. This may be movement, or the reading of the way technical skills are performed, giving a clue or direct inference about what will likely happen and thus the ability to Anticipate.

Add to these environmental variables and we see there are numerous factors to consider. The better you achieve this, or learn the possible outcome, the more chance you have of choosing and performing the correct response. So, we will look at what skills and information can help us achieve this.

Anticipation is an overlooked skill not given enough attention at most levels of sport. It is often trained as an adjunct to another skill rather than being treated, as I suggest, as one of the five major performance aspects within RACER. Getting better at Anticipation can determine the outcome of any game. Far more than a simple question of 'wait, look and react to whatever comes my way', the ability to Anticipate an opponent's play by perceiving their Choices or actions in advance, just prior to or as soon as possible after their acts occurs, is a multi-faceted and essential skill to develop.

While being Ready is achievable with concentration, grit and determination, Anticipation significantly ups the stakes. It requires more complex cognitive processing involving elements of intuition, and even a possibly mystical or metaphysical sense of what is about to happen.

"She's got eyes in the back of her head," and "how on earth did he see that coming?" might be our reaction when highly skilled performers or opponents pull off amazing feats of athleticism. But a closer look will reveal that players at the top of their game are able to pick up advanced visual cues from an opponent's movements, both bodily and positionally, as well as the actions of any player or players in their own team.

Such perception and visual acuity are used to inform and improve their Choices, which in turn affects their Execution.

Gretzky the Great - See you later, alligator

While researching this edition of the book, I looked for examples of sportspeople with great Anticipation. After hours of research, I came across someone I had read about many times, whose autobiography I had read, and who I always admired as a great sportsperson. I was thrilled to read and find out how important Anticipation was for him, in matches, practise, and learning.

My title is really a misnomer, as Wayne Gretzky, as a National Hockey League (NHL) player, was anything but 'great'. It is well known that his size, strength, and even speed were unimpressive compared even to the generally good ice hockey player.

But no one has the records he has. In fact, Gretzky stands like very few others, as a truly great and undisputed untouchable of his sport.

Take one stat. Gretzky is the only player ever to score 200 points in a season. And he did that four times! At his retirement in 1999, he held 61 NHL records, 40 regular season records, 15 playoff records, and six All Star records. Phew!

From a RACER point of view, the lesson is his ability to Anticipate. It's true that he had incredible stamina, but he did not have other physical attributes usually associated with the greats.

He is known to be one of the smartest ever players in the game. He understood and read the game well, so that he could consistently Anticipate what would happen, where the puck would be, and thus - incredibly - be in the right place at the right time, most of the time.

His coach at Edmonton Oilers, Glen Sather, said "He was so much more intelligent. While they were using all this energy trying to rattle his teeth, he was just skating away analyzing things."

In *Gretzky: An Autobiography*, he notes that, when people said he had a sixth sense, this was nonsense. "I've just learned to guess what's going to happen next. It's Anticipation."

After describing some practises and learning to Anticipate, Gretzky contends - as is my point in this chapter - "Who says anticipation can't be taught?"

He describes how, at practices, his father would drill him on the fundamentals of smart hockey:

Him: "Where's the last place a guy looks before he passes it?"

Me: "The guy he's passing to."

Him: "Which means..."

Me: "Get over there and intercept it."

Him: "Where do you skate?"

Me: "To where the puck is going, not where it's been."

Him: "If you get cut off, what are you gonna do?"

Me: "Peel."

Him: "Which way?"

Me: "Away from the guy, not towards him."

I hope this example shows the importance and excitement one can attain if one sees the practicality and advice that follows in this chapter.

Sports scientists including Robin C Jackson (Loughborough University) and Andrew Mark Williams (University of Utah) acknowledge that a player's Anticipation skill, and the level of their expertise and performance, go hand in glove. Some even go so far as to say Anticipation is what distinguishes the professional from the amateur.

Types of Anticipation

The most key skill in Anticipation is the ability to visually pick what your opponent is doing, as quickly as possible, so you can react and make your Choice. I call this direct involvement Anticipation.

An example could be taken from these two side-by-side pictures of me having just delivered a serve: which is going out wide to the advantage court, and which one is aimed down the centre?

Mike serving ball on racket   *Mike serving racket turned over*

The answer is that in the picture on the left, the ball is going down the centre as the hips and shoulders have rotated early and the racket has come around the ball, taking it down the middle of the court. The right photograph shows less rotation of the hips, and the racket face has hit on the inside of the ball, as you can see from the internal rotation of the forearm. Top players will easily pick up this cue.

There are other important factors such as secondary Anticipation, where you are more concerned about general movement and positional play. I will discuss three types of Anticipation, primarily on direct involvement Anticipation, i.e., what your opponent is going to Execute, for which you need to make an immediate decision. For example, judging the spin on the ball, where the ball is going, where they will pass, make a break for the line, grab your arm or hit you. I will also include what I call 'secondary Anticipation movement', as well as environmental factors.

Mastering Old Master Time

"Speed is often confused with insight. When I start running earlier than the others, I appear faster."

– Johan Cruyff

The beauty of good Anticipation is that it gives us more time to move into position and react, and so more time to make a potentially better Choice.

Reaction time can be placed on a scale from barely any time, to quite a bit of time. So sometimes we have a reasonable amount of time, for example, at a throw-in or preparing for a corner in field sports, while on other occasions we need the fastest and most intuitive Anticipation possible. Fencing and table tennis require lightning-fast Anticipation.

Within each sport, the time we have for Anticipation can vary. For example, you have much less time to Anticipate a fast ball in cricket than a slow, looping ball delivered by a spin bowler. Likewise, within sports the Anticipation time, as well as the skills required in different periods, moments and situations, can vary. Thus, the spin bowler mentioned above may deliver a quicker ball or vary their flight.

But no matter what the response time required is, good Anticipation gives us an advantage and, where sometimes split decisions make a big difference, it's the difference between success and failure in micro or macro situations, i.e., specific moments or in the general scheme of events. It is understanding and acting on the **conjunctive dimension** that is revelatory, i.e., the magic link, which is unique and can make such an impact on you or your team's performance.

The following diagram shows the different time frames when we Anticipate, focusing on tennis shots in this instance (where '1' = less time, '10' = more time). We need to work on each element to develop rounded Anticipation skills.

Anticipation Time Graph (Tennis):

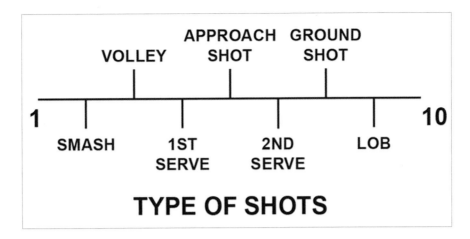

The Magic Link

The secret lies not ONLY in Anticipation itself, but in understanding that Anticipation is the link in the chain of causal events. One of the most important aspects of Anticipation is the fact that in sport it is one of the catalysts and key to success.

In this book, an important understanding to take away is its role in the RACER system, i.e., it is the conjunctive dimension where we really get value. So, while I may point out new perspectives and angles to view Anticipation, realising that Anticipation helps you make the Choice, and not just its role for Execution, is where part of its major significance lies.

Thus, it's not that we are Ready and suddenly we Choose. We Choose because after we are Ready, we Anticipate and then we can make our Choice. This may seem obvious, but as mentioned before, I have observed enough coaching and heard well-respected pundits who, in their comments, clearly miss out on this link.

For example, "What a bad pass" – but often the pass looks bad because the team-mate wasn't Ready or didn't Anticipate the pass. So, they look at the Choice but don't track back this sequence of causality.

Often coaches do exercises and drills where there is very little variation and the Choice is a mechanical reaction, if one could even call it a Choice! It's just, "Do this and do that". But in the live moment of sport, Anticipation work is needed to help and allow us to be aware of and make better or different Choices.

Move Towards the Ball, Not at The Ball

Another of my revelatory ideas in Anticipation refers to the movement and positioning of the feet and body. Anticipation is not just the ability to determine – to varying degrees – what is likely to happen to the ball or movement of players or opponents around you, but the ability to get yourself into the correct physical and mental state to be able to Execute your Choice, or to deal in the most appropriate way with movement or positional play of other players.

When I watch coaches in various sports shouting, "You are too close or too far from the ball" (or an opponent) – yes, maybe so. But why, and how can the moment be improved? It is understanding this, i.e., Anticipatory perceptual distance, that players will improve. Thus, moving towards the ball, not at the ball, or at the right pace and time if at an opponent. I term this 'Anticipatory movement, distancing and timing'. So, Anticipation is also about judging distance and the movement towards the object. This area in my experience is not emphasised enough or with the right understanding anyway.

Super Bowl Magic

A great example of Anticipatory movement occurred during one of the world's biggest sporting events, the Super Bowl, which in 2014 saw New England Patriots take on Seattle Seahawks.

There were 26 seconds left with the Patriots leading the Seattle Seahawks 28-24, but the Hawks had the ball yards from the touchline, knowing they would win the game with one rush, or a pass and catch. At this point the Hawks had a crucial Choice to make, with the latter option being the more spectacular, lower percentage play.

The Pats had to defend with all their RACER skills to prevail. But, in this example, the first two aspects are vital and show how important the sequence of RACER is. They must be totally dynamically Ready, then Anticipate the Hawks' play.

It is so difficult to Anticipate correctly in that instant – but the Pats had practised their defence for this potential eventuality pre-match, Anticipating this possible scenario. Malcolm Butler, who would make the crucial interception, was on the sidelines before the play began. Head coach of the Pats, Bill Belichick, Anticipated that the Hawks would opt for this particular pass-play, and sent Butler on.

The key element here was the Anticipation of the Pats' coaching staff in reading the potential play, as well as Butler himself, in Anticipating and then Executing the interception of Russell Wilson's pass, securing his legendary status with the Pats faithful in the process.

Post-match commentators and analysts were beside themselves at the Hawks' play call. With one of the most unstoppable running backs in the NFL on their roster, Marshawn Lynch, many thought they had made the wrong call. Though, of course, hindsight is a wonderful thing.

But credit must also go to the Pats for doing their homework and displaying, on the day, incredible Anticipation and Execution.

Mo Fará-Bulosa

Another good example is Mo Farah's rise from perennial 'also-ran' to the undisputed king of middle-distance running, which I believe came partly due to his improved tactical Anticipation. There are many great examples, but I choose a wonderful performance from the 10,000m final at the 2017 World Championships.

Knowing the Kenyans, who had the largest number of athletes in the final, could try to block him out, Mo started well away from them, keeping out of trouble at the back of the field.

Just after halfway, Mo Anticipated that the medal contenders would break away so joined the leading pack. So, while picking up his pace he Anticipated when to make his move, and who his key rivals were.

Then, with four laps remaining, he let his rivals know he was strong and still full of running, taking the lead. They subsequently fell for his bait, worried about his renowned finish and tried to push a bit too hard in reclaiming their positions at the front of the field.

With 600m to go, Mo took the lead, setting the pace he wanted. He was now in control of the race as they neared the final bend. Perfectly positioned on the inside, he suddenly accelerated. Although his opponents Anticipated a burst of pace they didn't know when that would be – and by then Mo was away, the gold medal his – again.

Watching any race that he's in is a fascinating study in this area of Anticipation. While I have watched him many times on television, my two live experiences of him – once at the London Olympics 2012 and at an international Diamond League meeting in Birmingham – really opened my eyes.

Feeling and seeing the action, and the way he moved, and thought, helped me appreciate his incredible understanding of his opponents and the Anticipatory strike skills he uses.

Side Effects

In addition, by Anticipating well, you could affect your opponent's Execution. Your movement and positioning can catch their eye or at least make them think harder which, in effect, puts mental pressure on them.

Thus, Anticipation is not just the ability to recognise or read a situation, but also to move into the best position.

Anticipation: The Hidden Secret

Many coaches take Anticipation for granted and place too much focus and emphasis on Execution. This is due to a combination of factors. Foremost, Execution has always been the 'star' of the show, being the most visible and easy to analyse.

Being good players themselves, coaches may neglect the less obvious, but essential, aspect of Anticipation. This weakness is then exacerbated by often not having the full understanding and knowledge to teach these Anticipation skills. The same applies to commentators who also tend to focus primarily on Execution.

Easy Tap In?

During the 2018 football World Cup in Russia, the Uruguayan superstar Luis Suarez scored what the commentator described as 'an easy tap in' against Saudi Arabia.

Of course, such superficiality stupefies me. Trust the pundits to trivialise or totally ignore the reason behind the 'easy' goal: superb Anticipation skills.

My first reaction to the goal was to note Suarez's incredible speed of movement and clinical finish. Then, when I watched in slow motion, my RACER thoughts and instincts kicked in. Suarez's Ready position was dynamic, and I noted how intently he watched the ball and intuitively Anticipated it arriving at where he had Anticipated. This allowed him to get onto the ball like a flash when the right moment arrived.

This one-dimensional commentary, which is not unusual, unfortunately made Suarez's goal look easy, while in fact it was his great Anticipation which earned him the goal.

Expect the Unexpected

Due to the vagaries of sport and the people playing it, Anticipation is not just a fixed occurrence, but is variable, depending on several factors. Sport can throw up some unexpected twists, adding to the intrigue of possibilities that need to be Anticipated.

Of course, sometimes it's impossible to Anticipate everything coming your way, hence terms like 'being thrown a curveball' and 'it came out of the blue'. But great players usually deal with the unexpected exceptionally well; likewise, the impressive level of consistency in dealing with the expected.

Factors Affecting Anticipation

There are three major factors affecting our Anticipation. They can – and do – overlap, but it is pertinent for didactic purposes to divide them:

1. Environmental and External Factors – Numerous outside factors influence our Anticipation and can change the entire nature of any game.
2. Personal Skills – Our senses, knowledge and intuition give us information, allowing us to react to opponents and even to predict what they are about to do.
3. Opponents – Be aware of what your opponent is doing tactically, what type of game they are playing and what changes they make during the action. If you have watched or played against your opponent before, it will help with your Anticipation.

Anticipation Factors Overlap:

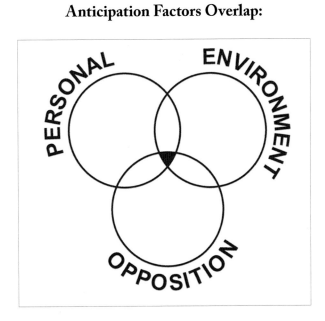

1. Environmental and External Factors

Weather conditions are of vital importance for Anticipation. How do wind, sun, temperature, rain, cloud and other weather conditions influence your performance and that of your opponent?

How the weather affects our Anticipation will change depending on the sporting discipline itself. For instance, indoor play means the weather outside is unimportant, but indoor conditions affect the sound and speed of play, demanding different skills in perception. In outdoor sports the weather is always considered pre-performance, but it may also require ongoing Anticipation throughout the match.

At higher levels, environment is taken very seriously in match and selection of players. For example, in cricket, if it's known the pitch will 'take' spin, then it's important to include one or two specialist spin bowlers. Or, in either rugby code, if the ball is very wet and slippery, using players with kicking strengths, or a kicking tactic, is a possibility.

One England rugby union skills coach worked with his players using a variety of rugby balls: large, small, dry, wet. This not only helps with improving players' coordination and handling skills but is a subtle form of kinaesthetic Anticipation. This involves carrying out physical skills rather than simply listening to information. It's also known as tactile learning.

Blowing Up A Storm

I was once teaching tennis to one of the senior consultants of a leading London hospital. She was playing with the wind behind her and, resultantly, too many of her shots were going out. The wind was strong enough to have her hitting, either lower, slower or with more spin – all of which are good suggestions when playing 'with' the wind. I gave this advice to her, asking her to try which of these would help her the most.

Unfortunately, she took my suggestions personally and let rip with a very defensive response. "Mike, you do not need to patronise and find excuses for me. I am a very successful woman and well able to deal with my mistakes without you having to blame the wind to make me feel better."

I was a bit taken aback and we played on while I thought how best to deal with this situation. I didn't feel it would be the greatest idea to get authoritative or didactic at that point.

After five minutes we swapped ends, which I regularly do (incidentally, one of the mistakes coaches and people practicing often make is to stay on the same side throughout a session). Of her first seven shots, five went into the net and the other two were hit very short.

She covered her face, then looked up and said: "Mike, I am so sorry, I just didn't realise how big an effect a breeze could have on the ball."

Blinded by the Light

Sunlight can be blinding, depending on the time of day, but if you use it to your advantage it can be very useful. For example, in rugby union or cricket, kicking or hitting the ball high will often unsight the catcher momentarily.

Or, if the sun is against your opponent in tennis, the tactic of hitting the ball in the air makes a smash for them extremely difficult. Using light as a tactic really comes to the fore under the glare of hundreds of thousands of lumens in today's big stadiums which cater for indoor and night games.

Some Like It Hot

A Test match in New Delhi, India with temperatures soaring above 40 degrees Celsius is a whole different ball game to playing at the Wanderers in Johannesburg, South Africa after a hailstorm has dropped temperatures by 10 degrees. Hot or icy conditions can be tremendously advantageous if you are used to them and know how to use the weather to squeeze an opponent.

If a team or player is battling under a boiling sun and showing signs of heat exhaustion, you can prolong play by slowing the tempo of the match down. An opponent in a singles tennis match may be tiring in the heat, so being a little more patient and moving them around could be a good tactical Choice.

During commentary for the 2017/18 Ashes Test cricket series in Australia, I heard England's former opening batsman, Geoffrey Boycott, encouraging the batsmen to make the fielders move around, to tire them out. The batsmen at the time were just playing safe, with the fielders not needing to do much running. So, Boycott's suggestion on a hot day was very apt. While not needing to take more risks, just having an awareness of moving the fielders around more throughout the day would have tired the fielding team and their bowlers, and thus increase the possibility of taking advantage of a tiring team later in the day.

Left Out in the Cold

Being unprepared for cold is guaranteed to ruin Anticipation for anybody. It stiffens our muscles and, in a strange way, our minds as well. We need to limber up extremely thoroughly and remember how cold continues to affect our muscle and respiratory functions throughout the game. Thus, our opponents may be slower and by Anticipating this, if we can accelerate that bit quicker, we can take advantage of their movement.

During breaks in play, muscles cool down faster in cold weather, so it's important to keep muscles moving. Players on the bench in team sports need to keep the blood and adrenaline pumping with frequent short jogs and stretching.

And don't forget to wear layers and to keep rehydrating. Just because it is cold, doesn't mean you're not losing liquids fast.

An important point to stress is what the cold does to the ball. The ball may bounce slower or be heavier. Whatever the case, awareness and Anticipation of this factor is important. In the winter, in my tennis classes I work on how to deal with low bouncing balls, practising this more so than in the summer. I have noticed this happen far more than people realise.

"It's my decision. Live with it": Referee/Umpire

It's important to Anticipate the temperament of an umpire or referee. Some officials are stricter than others and Anticipating this can help you make better Choices.

At higher levels, the coaches or managers meet the refereeing team before the game, so the players are often made aware of the style they will produce. Is the referee known to be quick to flash a yellow card? Is a tennis umpire known to award harsh penalty points for code violations such as temper tantrums?

Adapting to the Official

I was once coaching an Under-10s football team and it became clear very early on that the referee enjoyed the sound of his own whistle, blowing for almost everything. At half-time, with the score at 1-1, my main coaching point revolved around the referee: how to block without fouling, not to rush into the tackle, to let the opponent lose control of the ball by pressuring rather than using aggressive play. We went on to win 5-2, with two of our goals coming from free kicks

If we Anticipate a harsh referee or umpire, we can make tactical Choices to prevent unfair decisions in future.

The Crowd

*"Men, it has been well said, think in herds; it will be seen that they go mad
in herds, while they only recover their senses slowly, and one by one."*

– Charles Mackay

Would you rather have 60,000 people cheering for you, or baying for your blood? And how would you let this affect your mood and your play? The crowd factor plays a vital role in any competition and is often cited as being an 'extra' player when a team or individual enjoys the benefit of home advantage.

How does a team or individual player Anticipate the crowd factor and use it to their advantage? And if the fans are against you, how do you react? Do you crumble, or have you found a way of 'making peace' with the heckling, slagging and sledging that so often comes with away games?

Klopp The Kop

In a 2019 article about the return to prominence of Liverpool FC under Jurgen Klopp, one incident stood out.

At home, and 2-1 down to lowly West Bromwich Albion late in a Premier League game, the Reds scrambled a stoppage-time equaliser. After the final whistle the German made the decision to take his players towards The Kop and celebrate as though they'd recorded a famous victory.

This act was met by certain media and commentators with ridicule, questioning why Liverpool were reacting this way, 'celebrating' a point against the Baggies.

Yet as the article pointed out, this was Klopp winning over the crowd. The fans had started to feel a distance from the players and coaching staff. In response, here was Klopp coming out to them, offering a public thank you to the supporters for staying and backing the team until the end, showing how important that mutual support and effort was.

This turned out to be a huge turning point in the club's fortunes and is now seen as a crowd stroke of genius from Klopp.

There are many professional examples of how to play to home advantage, or to offset the disadvantage of playing away:

- In the early 2010s, the England rugby union team would arrive for home games by coach, stopping before the usual entrance so the squad could walk through the cheering crowd. This was more than just an excuse to bask in glory, but a sure way of galvanising England's support base.
- In cricket, paceman Mitchell Johnson wrecked the England cricket team's hopes of victory in the 2013/14 Ashes series, despite acknowledging he had a huge problem coping with opposition fans. He was teased and cajoled for his sometimes wayward 'radar' that caused him

to bowl too many wide balls. It was only after Johnson worked with a sports psychologist to deal with the anticipated 'English' crowd problem that he really became a success.

Letting the crowd strike a raw nerve can be prevented if you've Anticipated that you're in for punishment from a loyal home base. So, what can be done to minimise the psychological warfare that will be meted out by opposition supporters, and how can it be turned to our advantage?

Visualising crowd negativity by seeing yourself above the masses can help block out the biased and unnerving 'comments from the peanut gallery'. In fact, Novak Djokovic, who succumbed to crowd pressure in the Wimbledon final of 2013 against Andy Murray, had the same crowd situation in the 2019 final against Roger Federer. This time he had a tactic: he pretended the crowd was cheering for him. I was fortunate to be at both matches and I can vouch for the incredible change in the body language of Djokovic from the Murray final.

Interpreting the noise as cries for help and moans of desperation might help refocus your attention on the game. Or imagine the cheering is for the goal you're about to score or the point you're about to win.

In counteracting the madness of an opposition crowd, being forewarned is certainly being forearmed.

The Surface – Expect the Unexpected

The playing surface of any sporting discipline affects the way we move. The question to ask is how this information and understanding of the surface will influence both our Anticipation and subsequent Choices.

In ball games, the surface can make the ball travel slower or faster, or it may bounce higher or lower than expected, making everything more unpredictable.

The ground may be heavy, so passes along the ground will have to be struck harder to find their target in games like football and hockey. If you play on a thick surface, it will be more taxing on your legs, so be prepared for this eventuality and change your training and tactics accordingly.

In non-ball sports such as snowboarding and water-skiing, motor racing, athletics and all equestrian sports, Anticipating tricky surface conditions – and training and planning accordingly – is often the deciding factor.

By Anticipating a bad bounce, a bumpy outfield or a sodden pitch, we alert our minds and reflexes to expect the unexpected.

2. Personal Skills

What can you do personally to improve your Anticipation? For this, we must focus on the use of our senses to detect as much as we can from sound movements of both body and playing equipment, e.g. racket or bat.

The most important sense in sport is obviously sight. If you look at the right place at the right time, you can pick up the most important information from your opponent, and thus have knowledge about what's likely to happen next. Advanced players acutely watch their opponent's body position and movement in a specific sequence and manner, to pick up the slightest bit of information before contact or release. The critical moment is Anticipating the release or contact itself, as this is the actual Execution of your opponent or even team member. But without the extra pre-Execution information and awareness, it would be both too late and difficult to constantly Anticipate well.

So, in football, we watch the ball, but are also Ready for one of the feet to kick or move the ball. If you become mesmerised or react to step-overs (where the player pretends to move the ball), you will be fooled. Watch the feet as well as the ball.

As a schoolboy, I once played against a South Africa hockey international and was left aghast when one of my mates, an excellent defender, followed the Springbok's stick, rather than the ball. He ended up moving in totally the wrong direction. After the game, the Bok showed us how to do the trick, and how to avoid it being done to us. It was all to do with Anticipation.

Each sport has its own peculiar Anticipation requirements and skills. Thus, in tennis and table tennis you need to Anticipate the opponent putting topspin or slice on the ball, and how much spin. Or decide whether they are hitting a flatter shot.

In cricket, spin bowlers and fast bowlers offer different amounts of speed and movement. Without being able to detect this, the batsman is just guessing where the ball might be going.

Awareness of what is likely to happen, based on the situation and where the player is, can also be improved.

I am amazed at how many times I watch people heading the ball in football, with players often waiting to see what will happen. It duly becomes a 50/50 ball, but it shouldn't be the case. If you can roughly Anticipate the possible area of the ball's flight, get into that area. Players can only head a ball so far!

Looking Is Not Seeing, Listening Is Not Hearing

The speed and accuracy with which we watch and Anticipate an opponent's actions determine what the quality of our response will be. This ability to use visual clues accurately, and interpret an opponent's kinetic movements and split-second decisions, gives a distinct advantage. Let's also not forget sound and the importance of developing our hearing acuity. It's quite amazing how much we use our ears in any sport. Just try playing your sport with earmuffs on. This applies even more to sports where the ball makes a sound.

A great story is told of tennis legend Ivan Lendl on an indoor court refusing to play on whilst it was raining outside. When the umpire called the tournament director in to help resolve the issue, Lendl told him that it was not possible to play if he couldn't hear the ball.

Intuition

Intuition is the ability to have an inner sense of what is going to happen. The better the player, the more they tap into this rather mysterious quality.

Intuition works on a far more sophisticated and faster level than the cognitive analytical mind. The best way to describe this is in terms of technology. If a player has an app with all the data of experience and knowledge applied, in the heat of the moment this ability is faster than the normal mind, and thus they can make a decision most people are not able to implement.

3. Opponents

While not everyone has the luxury of scouting their opponents, there are still several Anticipation skills to use when sizing up the other side. Often you might play individuals or teams over several years, so it's a good idea to keep a journal and jot down a few notes. Or, if possible, speak to other people who have played or watched your opposition before. During the warm-up is also a good time to spot potential opposition weaknesses.

Another good suggestion is to learn and Anticipate something about your opponent in the warm-up. Once, preparing to play for my university in a table tennis match, I noticed the opposition player had a great backhand, until I slowed the ball down and it looked like he struggled with the change of pace and the slower ball. Sure enough, I started to use this shot in the match and his game fell apart. So, a great idea and a good time to Anticipate aspects of your opponent's game is during this period.

In training or social situations, an awareness and effort to work on and be aware of Anticipation, with a desire and determination to improve in this area will pay great dividends in the long run.

In Summary

Anticipation involves obtaining important information from the environment, your opposition and your own team members. Prior knowledge of opponents and situations, combined with personal skills including as many senses as possible, allows us to Anticipate events more productively, effectively and efficiently. The good news is that we can improve on all these aspects of Anticipation by becoming aware and working on them generally and specifically.

Coaches often ignore the intricacies and specifics of Anticipation as they take these skills for granted. Because they are adept and competent in this area, they don't appreciate the difficulty some people have in this regard.

It is Anticipation that distinguishes professionals from more casual players, which is more reason for us as coaches and aspiring pupils to teach and practice it.

Having considered my points in this chapter, your goal would be to use the information and explore where you or your team can improve, remembering that the Anticipation phase of the RACER system is the crucial link between being Ready and Choice.

Chapter 3

CHOICE

"To be, or not to be, that is the question."

- WILLIAM SHAKESPEARE, *HAMLET*

Consider these scenarios:

- Millions of people are watching you on TV. The roaring, 80,000-strong crowd goes deathly silent as you line up your penalty. Do you decide to go left, right or straight? It's a game-changing - and life-changing - moment.
- Your whole school is watching as you hurtle down the field towards the try line, ball in hand and seemingly chased by monstrous, bloodthirsty enemies. Do you cut inside, go outside or keep going straight? Your team is about to lose the game, or you are about to become a hero.
- It's Sunday morning in a run-down park. You're playing a grudge match against a friend when a man with a walking stick, two dogs and a cat stop to watch, momentarily distracting you. Your opponent is on the run and the dogs bark as the ball goes up in the air. Do you elect to go for the winner or play safe, the easier option, to get your concentration back?

There is one definitive common denominator in all three scenarios that could affect the outcome. All three characters are about to make a vitally important Choice.

Not all Choices, of course, have the latter significance. But what is clear is that we need to be making Choices. The more time we can create, the better we decide, the more control we have of our Choices, the more successful we or our team will be. Having gotten Ready and Anticipated well, we have now given ourselves the best chance of a good Choice. So, the third part of RACER is our Choice.

The Choice that cost Super Bowl 51

One occasion where Choice certainly mattered was Super Bowl 51. The Atlanta Falcons were an incredible 28-12 up in the Super Bowl Final against the much vaunted favourites, the New England Patriots. It was around 1am UK time and like many in my time zone, I went to bed thinking, "Game over!"

Then with 3:56 remaining, and the Falcons 28-20 up, Falcons quarterback Mat Ryan was sacked. The result led to an incredible finish and a win for the Pats.

From a RACER perspective, the Falcons made a shocking and perhaps hubristic Choice. The one Choice they had to make was to choose a play where a sack was not possible. They were still in field goal range. Any Choice had to allow them to go for the field goal, making it a two score game. With very little time left, that would have made it practically impossible for the Pats to come back and win.

The Choice should have been to run the ball, a much safer and more practical option at this stage of the match, compared to the risky throwing option. Once they were within range, the Choice had to be to kick for a field goal. Maybe they got too aggressive, too optimistic. The bottom line: the wrong Choices were made.

Plus, their kicker Matt Bryant had a 100% record from 40-49 yards, so the 35-yard kick was well in his range. The end result was a crushing and historic loss.

The first task is to map out what constitutes Choice. Once you have a clear view of the options, understanding and importance of Choice, then looking at your specific sport, prioritising and then working through the relevant areas is a key to success. Each sport has a variety of Choices, which is partly why sport is so intriguing – and so much fun.

First, Choice can be seen on a spectrum, from instantaneous to thinking and accessing, i.e., from reflex to considered.

Second, Choice can be divided into three broad categories: defence, neutral or attack. Within all three, one can make a Choice from low or high complexity or risk.

Thus, in defence you could just hit or kick the ball out of play and have no risk, or you can try and make a pass or dribble yourself out of trouble. This could be deemed as high risk, yet in both situations you are defending.

The following 'Categories of Choice' diagram shows the scale of each of the three Choices. '1' represents the lower scale with '10' being the extreme, whether defence or attack. When neutral gets to its maximum it, in fact, transitions to defence or attack.

Categories of Choice:

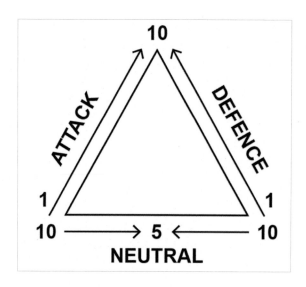

Neutral is the most stable aspect of Choice, i.e., the most commonly played of the three, and is usually the foundation of success. Having a sound and consistent foundation allows you to build towards attacking or build from a defensive situation. So, most of our Choices are neutral until the time comes to defend or attack.

Whether a time frame or a tactical Choice, we must remember that when you decide can relate to the Choice of your movement: where and if you should move, how fast you should go somewhere (support play and positional movement), or the actual Choice of what you want to physically Execute. You might want to Execute kicking, jumping, throwing, hitting, or perhaps a sudden acceleration, depending on your sport This includes, for example, when to suddenly accelerate in Karate, swimming, cycling, athletics, basketball, netball, etc. We could divide this into indirect Choice (movement) or direct Choice (pre-Execution).

The importance of the Choice in support play cannot be underestimated. I remember a commentary on a Barcelona football match during their heyday, circa 2014. One of the commentators remarked on the incredible ball skills of the players. The other commentator said: "Watch them when they haven't got the ball; look at how they move and run; this is what makes them so special." What a telling point that was.

The following story, in many ways, encapsulates the importance of Choice.

Choice Makes Champions

It's the quarter-finals of Wimbledon 2018 and Roger Federer is two sets to love and match point up against the huge-serving South African, Kevin Anderson. A few hours later, and the 'Federer Express' is on his way home.

In the semi-final against the equally massive-serving American, John Isner, Anderson slips on the ground six hours into the longest Grand Slam semi-final in history. Anderson intuitively uses his non-playing left hand to hit a great shot down the middle of the court. A shot down the middle is the safest one to hit as it gives your opponent less angle.

As he was on his backside, it is easy to understand and admire his instinctive Choice. A few points later and Anderson wins an unforgettable marathon match 26-24 in the deciding set.

Now for the final against one of the greatest players of all time, Novak Djokovic. The great Serbian player hadn't won a Grand Slam tournament in two years and had recently blown a match point in the Queen's Club final against Marin Cilic.

But a couple of wrong Choices, and missed shots from Anderson that had a clear possibility of success, let Djokovic off the hook. Anderson's failure to take advantage of his opponent's non-Choices ended his Grand Slam dreams. The key to the events was Choice. Anderson acknowledged this when he said in his press interview afterwards that on the big stage, the elite players make the right Choices and then Execute them properly.

Joan N. Vickers highlights the vital components of Choice in her 2007 book, *Perception, Cognition, and Decision Training: The Quiet Eye in Action.*

Vickers' system is designed "to improve the athletes' attention, anticipation, concentration, memory and problem-solving skills through practices where cognitive training is incorporated with physical and technical training. The overall goal is the development of an athlete who is able to make effective decisions under all the pressures of completion."

Vickers shows that Choice is not just about the action or Execution of hitting, kicking, passing, catching or tackling, but that movement is crucial as well: when to go forward, sideways or back, and when to move to certain positions.

Choice on the Big Stage

Manchester City manager Pep Guardiola, boss of arguably one of the most attractive footballing sides in the English Premier League era, constantly refers to Choices and the solution of problems. "My players have to make choices, they have to solve these problems," he said about match situations.

An 'Opportunity to be Thoughtful' – Southgate Chose Choice

In an article in the *Sunday Times* in 2017, David Walsh wrote about one of the reasons Gareth Southgate was chosen as England football manager in 2016. Southgate had realised that the English players "needed to think more about how they played and to embrace the challenge of becoming more tactically astute".

It's important to note that this was written before England's success at the 2018 World Cup in Russia.

Southgate duly set up situations where the players had to make Choices, and the pros and cons of each potential Choice would then be discussed and systematically worked through. In this way, the players were "given the opportunity to be more thoughtful and analytical in their approach to the game".

It shows the efficacy of Southgate's work and the effect of making Choices on and off the ball. Training for situations is vital and allows easier access and clarity of thought when it comes to making Choices under pressure situations.

England's remarkable run in Russia ended with them coming within 20 minutes or so of making their first final since 1966.

Former England rugby union coach, Sir Clive Woodward, instilled the acronym 'T-CUP' – short for 'Thinking Clearly Under Pressure' – in his players. In the heat of the game, players could now remind themselves to make clear-headed Choices and not cave into enormous pressure. T-CUP helped deliver tangible success in the form of the 2003 World Cup. Another excellent example of the importance of thinking under pressure occurred in the third Ashes Test of 2019, which saw one of the most exhilarating individual performances of all time.

As the game built to a finale, victory was slowly being taken away from the Australians. The pressure on their captain, Tim Paine, started to show, culminating with England needing eight runs to win. At this stage an LBW decision went against them. It was clear to everyone, including the bowler, that the umpire's decision was correct. But in a clear state of not thinking well under pressure Paine, for the sake of it, used up his last appeal – which he lost.

Then, with only two runs needed Ben Stokes was caught, in the view of most observers bar the umpire, right in front of his stumps, who inexplicably gave a not out decision. The Australians had no appeal left while TV replays showed it was clearly out. Had Paine not thought so recklessly earlier, not only would Australia have won the match, but they would have retained the Ashes with two Tests remaining.

It reminds me of one of my favourite lines from the film *Pretty Woman*, when Julia Roberts' character returns to a clothes store all dressed up and looking rich, having previously been turned away. She admonishes the sales team, who work on commission: "Big mistake. Big. Huge!"

T-CUP applies to all aspects of sport, but CHOICE is so pivotal that it is relevant here. With thorough preparation, the individual or team can keep the right focus, able to make the right decisions at the most pivotal, high-pressure moments.

The Pivotal Role of Choice

In all sports, whether you are striking, running, wrestling, kicking or moving into supporting defensive or attacking positions, you are always making continual Choices. This Choice will then influence your opponents and possibly your team-mates. Choice is right in the centre of RACER. It acts as the catalyst for the two elements before and after, thus playing a significant role in our success.

It is in our own hands or cognitive ability to decide the degree of difficulty of our Choice. As we have seen there are different scenarios of Choice, but the bottom line is that we must realise and take responsibility for – and work on – our skills and understanding of Choice.

The more difficult the Choice, the more challenging our subsequent Execution. Likewise, the easier our Choice, the more straightforward the Execution. Yet the rewards could be higher for the riskier Choice, or vice versa. The skill is to make the smarter and more appropriate Choice continually throughout the match.

Not all Choices are equal. Certain parts of a match are more pivotal than others. The Choice here is vital, and can decide the eventual outcome of a match. Elite sport is filled with glorious Choices as well as graveyard ones. There are legions of heroes and villains, all due to the right or wrong Choice being made at the most critical moment.

Take Your Pick

As you may know, in basketball you get three points if you get the ball through the hoop from outside the circle, and two points if you are inside. So in fact, ten shots of three points are worth 15 of two points. In effect, quite a lot more shots are needed if you go for twos and the game gets to scores of 80 plus.

Yet for some reason one season, possibly because of the marking or his extra patience, Michael Jordan hit a record number of two pointers. This was not arbitrary. Jordan made a clear and practical Choice that the two pointers would be the game winners.

Breaking Choice Down

Choices will depend on the type of sport and the way you want to play, i.e., aggressively, transitionally, or defensively. But what they all have in common is that there are usually options. Anyone can learn to make better decisions, as well as possess different game plans to use at the right time and place. The time factor in Choice is very important and it's amazing to watch great players. Not only do they look impressive, but they seem to have so much more time when in action. One reason they can do this, besides some natural ability, is the hours and hours practising studiously and intensely. Their minds, body movements, and reflexes allow them to make quicker, more appropriate, decisive Choices than others.

Finding Your Choices

Our Choices must always be weighed up with the reward value from whatever decision we make. Players and coaches within each sport must consider the following factors:

- What Choices are there to focus on? Break these down into ever smaller components, with each level of performance having different Choices, e.g., batting defensively in cricket, the serve for racket sports, controlling a moving ball.
- Positions within teams, e.g., in rugby union, the fly-half and back-line players.
- Team situations, e.g., the scrum in rugby, attacking and defensive set-ups at corners.

With good training, once players have been made aware of Choices, the coach should then set up situations which reinforce their tactical Choices.

As an example, within most racket games:

- Pace – How fast, medium or slow should we strike the ball?
- Place – Where should we strike the ball?
- Spin – Should we put on some topspin or backspin, or hit relatively flat?

In some racket sports, like squash and badminton, spin is less important than the pace and placement of the shot. Nevertheless, the aim of racket sports players is to decide on the best combinations of pace and place.

Choice of Style

After being beaten by Andy Murray for the first time, a peeved Roger Federer commented in a post-match interview that if the Scot was going to continue to play like that, he wouldn't win a Grand Slam. So, he changed his play and learned to be more aggressive with his Choice.

This shows the subtlety of Choice at higher levels. Federer was pointing out that to win the seven matches to clinch a Grand Slam, which he had already done numerous times, a player can't get away with a defensive mindset, which Murray did in that best-of-three-set match. Murray, if you watch his development, took this advice and to date has won three Grand Slams.

A 'Shotgun', A 'Horse Collar Tackle' Or A 'Pooch Punt'?

You don't have to know anything about American football, or its marvellous terminology, to realise how each team is broken down into specialist areas and that, within each of these, specific Choice skills are worked on.

The team is divided into offensive and defensive players, plus a kicker, usually the quarterback, who receives the ball the most often and thus needs to know exactly when, where and how to pass, run or kick.

In defence, teams require Choices which are dependent on where the opponent throws or kicks the ball, and what players are tackling the attacking team. Choices require movements away from defenders, as well as offensive team players effectively blocking defenders.

RACER helps make people aware that Choice in all areas needs to be considered and worked on within its own rights as an essential skill. Thus, do drills and exercises where Choice is explained, emphasised and practised. I have watched many practises from all sports, and I don't believe I have seen enough of working on the skill Choice. Much is by rote and instruction; thus, this vital cognitive decision-making skill is dormant. Over the years I have rectified this in my own teaching and practise of Choice is prevalent. More on practise of Choice skills later.

The two stories below show the different sides of Choice. On the one hand, limit your Choices for efficiency of thought and practicality of Execution; on the other hand, be creative in making your Choices and decisions, which creates better players.

"Even the best make time for me!"

In my younger days, I was not averse to teaching tennis for up to 12 hours a day. Yes, those were the days! On one occasion, a pupil called to say she was running late and so I headed to my office to wait for her.

Almost immediately, a lady walked in asking for a lesson. She was from Australia and was only in town for a few days. I told her that, unfortunately, I was booked up. The lady became exasperated and said: "Even the top coaches back home always find a time for me, even when they're busy."

I replied that I could only work so many hours in a day. But then a thought struck me, and I relented, saying: "Okay, if you tell me something interesting from one of these so-called 'top' coaches, I will find an hour for you." She thought carefully and then told me about the former ladies' world No.3, Amanda Coetzer.

One of the 'great coaches' had worked with Amanda on one of her weaknesses, the volley. Not that this was the most important part or shot of her game, as the live-wire South African was 5 feet 2 inches tall. But she was a very good doubles player and enjoyed volleying. She was losing too many points when she attempted the shot at the net through a poor or misplaced volley.

When they discussed and looked at her volleys they noticed on both backhand and forehand she had a variety of Executions; in a sense, too many Choices. So, the coach advised her to cut her Choices down to the best volley on each side, and one alternative for each. By doing this she was able to not only improve on the specific volley but shortened her thinking time and focus on the Execution more thoroughly. The result was a huge improvement on her winning percentage when volleying.

Sometimes, less Choice = less complication

In the same vein, former US tennis player Mardy Fish was once asked what skills he was working on when he had just entered the top 10 in the world to achieve his high ranking. His reply was by making better Choices.

How Can RACER Help You Improve Your Choice?

I recall a pupil once saying to me: "Choose? Phew, I don't have time, I'm just trying to hit the damn ball." While the comment was made in jest, maybe this was a valid point.

There are three principles to consider here:

- Learning how to proactively improve our Choices
- Being aware that good Anticipation leads to good Choice
- Breaking down Choices into units and building relevant options

RACER helps merely by alerting us to the cognitive aspect of Choice. We are in control of our Choices, and it is up to us to be proactive. There are various ways to proactively improve our Choices. First, make the players aware of the possibilities, and then work on them. The level of the player or team is important, as Choice possibilities will vary. Whatever these may be, there should be default Choices ('Plan A'), with other possibilities on hand.

An increasingly common Choice for a defender in top-level professional football is to pass the ball and play themselves out of trouble. At a lower level, players don't always possess the required skills to do this, and safely kicking the ball out of play is a better Choice.

In tennis, if you are an average-to-good player, a defensive shot high down the middle of the court is a good Choice. However, at the top level Choice in general, even in defence, needs to be of a high quality, otherwise the opponent easily takes advantage and usually wins the point. So, the first step is knowledge, i.e., knowing what your Choices actually are - the range of possibilities

With practice, this knowledge becomes more automatic when under pressure.

Secondly, the RACER sequence has made you aware that Choice is more successful if there is an awareness that good Anticipation leads to Choice. Here, it is important to work on different scenarios that can occur due to Anticipation.

Thus, in cricket, batsmen might work on their Choice of calling for a run. When a batter hits the ball, they must Anticipate the speed of the fielder, the distance the ball has been hit, the field conditions and the speed of your batting partner, before Choosing whether to call a run or not. Good Anticipation of these situations and other factors will help players make the right Choice to run, wait or stay, when in high-pressure situations.

World Cup Chokers

A great example of poor Anticipation and Choice under pressure occurred in the semi-finals of the 1999 Cricket World Cup between South Africa and Australia. Four days earlier, in a round-robin match, Australia had scraped a win with two balls to spare in a thriller to qualify; but four days later, the semi-final got even better.

Australia scored a modest 213 and in reply, South Africa were soon struggling until, with a few overs to go, one of the greats of one-day hitting, Lance Klusener, let rip and brilliantly gave South Africa a chance, leaving then needing nine runs off the last over but with only one wicket left.

The crowd went crazy as Klusener bashed the Australia bowler Damien Fleming for two successive fours of the first two balls of the over, meaning that only one was needed to win with four balls left and the odds heavily stacked in their favour.

Allan Donald, a feared bowler rather than batsman, and thus with less skill and awareness of running between the wickets, charged off for a run off the third ball, even though Klusener had mis-hit to a close fielder and hadn't called for a run, and nearly got himself run out scurrying back. Now, he loses his composure, i.e., he doesn't Recover. Klusener himself is unsettled: let's not forget this is the last few seconds of the World Cup semi-final!

Next ball, Klusener unwisely hits a similar shot, but now calls for the run. Donald doesn't hear as he is in a panic, then realises he needs to run. He drops his bat accidentally and is run out – it's all over. South Africa are all out for the same score as Australia – but because of their defeat four days earlier, Australia go through to the final, and eventual victory over Pakistan.

What should have been both practised and performed was that the senior batsman (Klusener) should have calmed the other batsman down – getting Ready. The next part was to Anticipate, in this case, to watch the batsman's lips. Listen for a "yes" or "no" call, and Execute the Choice, i.e. run for your life!

These are the finer details that professionals, I presume, would be working on; well, especially if they used the RACER system.

In sports such as table tennis and tennis, where spin is constantly relevant, a player's Choices depend on accurate Anticipation of bounce and speed variation. So, working on Anticipation and the following Choice is very important.

The Glory of Rising Phoenix: Split-second Choosing

How would you like to be in a wheelchair, with you and your adversary both holding sharp sabres, and have to Choose to lunge, parry, or riposte? Well, this is the moving story of the incredible Bebe Vio, with the moniker 'Rising Phoenix'. One day an eleven-year-old fencing prodigy, the next day in hospital for 104 days with meningitis. Then, to save her life, her forearms were amputated. She seemed to be progressing towards recovery when both legs were amputated from the knee. So when she won gold in her wheelchair in Rio 2016, you can imagine the explosion of emotion. I know from the couple of sessions that I tried that fencing is a tough sport. While most fencers would have to be precise and astute in RACER principles, to perform these skills in a wheelchair adds another layer of complexity. One comment that Bebe makes about being in a wheelchair is that she needs to be super Ready for the blade. Without this skill, the ability to make a Choice and Execute your move is even harder.

In football or hockey, to Choose to make a tackle, you need your eyes focused in the right area. Your focus is on watching the ball, yet you also need peripheral vision to help with your reactions and to choose the right moment when committing to the tackle. Watching Cristiano Ronaldo bamboozle opposing defenders with his step-overs is fascinating, and shows how difficult it is, even for the most highly skilled players, to make the right Choice of when to make their move as they try to stop the Portuguese wizard known as *El Comandante*.

Finally, once we are aware of the plethora of Choices, we start breaking them down into units. We should work on the important ones first and then build a relevant number of options.

Progressions are a good way to improve Choice. Make sure that the skills involved to Execute the Choice have been developed. Work on basic scenarios where these Choices occur. Training under pressure and scoring is added until this aspect is more automatic and becomes natural. Once the pupil or team has achieved that skill and can Execute the Choice, the coach then increases the degree of difficulty. Ideally, you finish off by testing the skill or Choice as if in a live, real-match situation.

A practical example might be when the coach picks an aspect of Choice such as direction. In racket sports, the coach could hit to the player who then verbalises their Choice, i.e., hit left, right or centre. Or colours can be placed on the court and they select the colour that they wish to direct the ball at. This is now performed non-verbally.

The progression then is to perform the skill in a general rally situation, perhaps adding serves, scoring points and finally a game with as much pressure as possible to feel the skill has become more instinctive. Andy Murray, for example, has forfeits and various ideas that bring out the competitive element and increases the tension in sessions.

I have seen enough people coming to my sports lessons for the first time to make me realise that many just want to be able to hit the ball as fast and as well as they can, or to pass the ball to the best player or bowl as quickly as they can. They have not yet been made aware enough of the options and skills required to maximise their Choices. For instance, the Choice to slow the game down and vary their pace, how to construct a point or be patient in a build-up. Knowing what the various options and Choices are helps them to improve.

One of my catchphrases is: "Your best shot is not your best shot".

In other words, trying to play above yourself, at the peak of what your ego tells you, is not pragmatically your best shot, aka Choice.

Three Choice Tips

- Practise making decisive Choices
- Rarely change your mind
- Have a back-up Choice

The Overrule Principle

Many coaches do drills with their pupils in which they are set tasks. You kick one ball here then run there, you hit three shots towards one area and the fourth you aim for the opposite side. The point here is that Choice, such a vital part of the process, has in fact been left out. As mentioned previously, there are certainly times when this is fine with the objective of, say, patterns of play in mind that need to be drilled. But this rote, mechanical drilling is used too often and, in the past, even by yours truly.

I thus introduced and coined the term 'overrule principle'. While the player understands the importance of the drill, they are aware of making a Choice and that there is a possibility of 'overruling' the set Choice, thus really bringing the process of Choice into play. Here are some examples to illustrate this:

Example 1 – A player crosses the ball and another shoots at the goal in any sport, e.g., football, hockey. So, whatever the cross (high or low, quick or slow, straight, ahead or back), the player goes for goal but, in fact, sometimes this is not the correct Choice. Sometimes it might be better to pass it back to the crosser, who can then try to improve on their first attempt, i.e., making a better shooting opportunity.

Example 2 – Place a cone outside the circle of attack in a baseball court. Players sprint up to the cone and the coach shouts "left" or "right", and the player goes the way instructed. But to keep making decisions, the player can in fact go the opposite way to the side called for, or even make a circle around the cone. In effect, the player is overruling the drill and making their own Choice = the 'overrule principle'.

As part of my coaching, I challenge pupils to think for themselves in practise situations as much as possible. Being aware of the Choices at hand, they know that they can make their own decisions. By keeping the Choice mindset active, the skill to choose is always present and practiced.

This is preferable to the rote activity of just following instructions, which is not realistic for live match situations, as the England Rugby Union team found out in the World Cup final in Japan in 2019.

The Hidden Cs

Although 'C' stands for Choice in the RACER breakdown, as time has gone by, I've realised that there are other pertinent words that apply to the letter 'C' as well. I call these supporting words 'the hidden Cs' because, as already mentioned, 'C' is in the middle of the RACER system. It is also pertinent that these hidden Cs are both important in themselves and help bind the system together.

So the following are all important factors in sporting success and I refer to them often and as appropriate. What follows is a very brief summary of each one:

- Concentration – The ability to stay focused on the skill at hand, and to stay in the moment. Choose to focus on your present aim, try not to get caught up in the possible distractions around you, or even those inside your head.
- Confidence – Believe as much as you can in your Choice. As W. Timothy Gallwey points out in his classic book, *The Inner Game of Tennis – The Ultimate Guide to the Mental Side of Peak Performance,* there are two selves: the conscious and the subconscious, or the critical and the doing. We don't want the doubting and critical self to interfere with and block our innate abilities. Confidence summed up is just feeling good about what we are doing.
- Composure – The ability, whether attacking or defending, to Execute on the run, e.g., to return a difficult shot, to not get ruffled, to display a sense of composure and clear headedness. I can honestly say that when running to take a difficult shot or even rushing in to Execute a potential winner, I bring the word composure to mind and it really helps me.
- Control – Keeping command of mind and body. Whether there have been good points and bad, correct and poor decisions, we must try to stay in control of the process.
- Commitment – Whatever the situation, give your best, keep your intensity and integrity. Remember your motivation, pride and commitment to team-mates, coaches, spectators and family. This will give you a mindset in which you have no regrets, just very positive feelings for what you have put into your sport.

The hidden Cs are meaningful and insightful words that back up and compliment the effectiveness of the Choices we make. While Choice is a form of analytical functioning of the brain, the hidden Cs add an emotional and psychological aspect to this very important stage of the process.

Words are psychological anchors, reference points and motivators, which help ensure that Choice is well supported and backed up.

In Summary

You can't avoid making Choices. It is very important to practise and learn the art of this skill, rather than subsume Choice within Executing. Becoming proficient at Choice allows you to be in a better state of mind and to be proactive, as opposed to reactive and rushed, when it comes to making the inevitable Choice.

It's important to know the range of possibilities you have when Choosing, and to be aware of your individual or team's skill level. Also, be mindful of what the objective is, and that you need to improve the quality and type of Choice.

Practising making the correct Choice in different ways is more conducive to learning than mere rote repetition.

Choice is the nucleus of RACER. It is the moment you launch your claim on a point or on any phase of a game, so make sure it's a good one. Don't be overly critical or doubtful, and know the one thing you can control is your effort.

We want to play sport with a clear, focused and happy mind, so if you get overloaded, it will affect your performance. By playing predominantly within your Choice comfort zone, you are far more likely to Execute successfully than by going overboard. It is very interesting to remember that most matches are not won by incredible and amazing Executions, but by consistent all-round performance and pragmatic Choices.

In any given situation in any sport, we must make continual decisions: when, where and how fast to run, where and how hard to kick, hit or throw a ball, where to position ourselves in relation to an opponent, how much risk to take, etc.

In all sports, whether you are in the striking, kicking, supporting, defensive or attacking position, the Choice you make is almost inextricably linked to your Execution.

The best players often minimise their Choices, even though they can consider and utilise far more options than lower-skilled players. This is because they can decide – often instantaneously – on the one or two options that will yield the best results. Their ability to sift through the plethora of Choices and consistently select the best one is what makes them so good.

We must learn from the best and put into practise as best we can what they do: in this case their Choice. Watch why and when they Choose to do certain things. On that basis, look at how that applies to us within the range of our skill ability and context. By learning even a few lessons from them, our decision-making and thus successful application within our sport will improve.

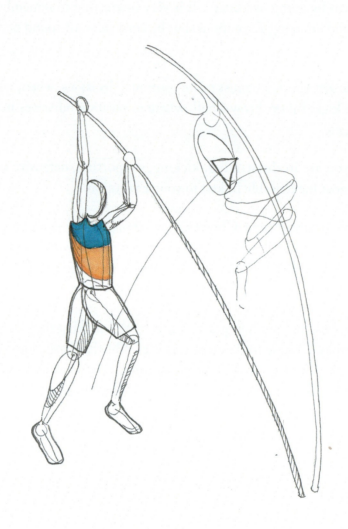

Chapter 4

EXECUTION

"A really great talent finds its happiness in execution."
- Johann Wolfgang von Goethe

After we have made our Choice, we must now Execute to the very best of our ability. The mental and physical demands of every game in all sports comes to an explosive point at the moment of Execution.

Good Execution requires a strong, focused body and mind. While this might seem obvious, for several reasons it's not always as simple as it seems.

The better the player or the team, the more likely they are to Execute their Choices successfully. But everyone, from beginners to the most advanced players or teams in the world, sometimes gets it horribly wrong. The embarrassment happens to everyone. I remember three classic examples of how even the best can make incredible errors in Execution.

Example 1: Baseball – In researching this book, I came across a sequence of errors that was probably one of the worst cameos of poor professional sporting Execution I have witnessed. The San Diego Padres were playing the Los Angeles Dodgers in Major League Baseball. With a very ordinary hit to midfield, the fielder can make an easy stop with a chance for a tag at first base. But with a horrendous throw, the first baseman can stop it. He then throws badly, which is not stopped. Then same again with the third throw! And to finish off, the last throw is off mark. Quite unbelievable to watch. A commentator rated this as probably the worst throw of the year.

Example 2: Golf – Another memorable failure to Execute came in golf at the Masters in 2016 when Jordan Spieth incredibly birdied the last four holes of the front nine, opening a four-shot lead. The closest person to him on the leaderboard was little-known Englishman Danny Willett. With nine holes to go, social media went crazy, and to all intents and purposes was declaring Spieth the winner.

Then Spieth's Execution went horribly wrong and his imperious form disappeared. He bogeyed the 10th and 11th holes and then at the 12th he played what must rank as one of the worst holes a top-10 player in Masters history had ever played. Spieth needed seven strokes to complete his quadruple bogey. He never got his groove back. His Execution had let him down and the defence of his title was over.

Example 3: American Football – In the 2017 Super Bowl, the Atlanta Falcons were 28-3 up against the New England Patriots. I was watching on television in the UK but went to bed before the end of the game, thinking it would be almost impossible for the Patriots to make a successful comeback. When I woke up the next morning, I received news of one of the greatest comebacks in National Football League history. The Patriots won 34-28.

What had happened was an amalgamation of RACER goods and RACER bads from both sides, with the Patriots doing all the good, including completing two of arguably the greatest Execution throws and catches in NFL history. In every respect, and by all accounts, the resurgent Patriots had improved their Execution and come out on top.

The point of these examples is to illustrate that Execution is not merely the next stage and the obvious and inevitable event after Choice. Even the best players make mistakes. The skill, concentration and sheer tenacity needed to perform consistently under pressure has led to some of the biggest upsets in sport.

We need to learn or improve on our ability to move from Choice to Execute. By understanding what Execute entails and with good practise and training, we can get our Execution matching our Choice – and this is the aim.

When you hear a post-match interview in which a player or manager says that everything went to plan, they are, in effect, saying that we executed our planned tactical Choices.

Another fascinating take on Execution comes from the amazing Peter Crone. Crone is a world renowned and fantastic mental coach for sport as well as life. He works on the psychology team for the Arizona Diamondbacks, the US National League baseball team.

When Crone talks about baseball, he says it is a sport of failure, pointing out that the top players miss seven out of ten shots. That's quite amazing if you think about it! Most people, including myself, would not have thought the best would have so many misses.

This means that top players have to be able to deal with failure, and not let it affect them personally. Crone says that failure to Execute is an event, not a person. In fact, he breaks it down further to say that failure is just something that happened. You missed the kick, you dropped the ball, and so on. Understanding this process helps to keep the right frame of mind at the right time, place and situation. When the situation and all factors are right, the person - over time - is far more likely to succeed.

Otherwise, the ego gets involved and reinforces inadequacy if we look or take on board events in a negative or personal way. Crone's insight is a very deep and useful tool to help one succeed in this fourth element of RACER.

I will go on to discuss some of the great Executions in sport in terms of the positive significance to the match. Perhaps, with the knowledge obtained in this chapter, you will have a better appreciation of these great Executions and be inspired to do the same.

The Time Has Come!

So, what is Execution? It is a combination of the physical and psychological components of an individual who performs a physical action.

How you hold your physique and shape or form are key factors, as well as what's going through your mind just before – and during – Execution. There is no tactical aspect as such – this should have happened in Choice. Execution is about doing. You either do, or you don't!

Both aspects are fundamental to improving our Execution, and yet the psychological side is often ignored. After thousands of hours attending courses, I've noted that the solutions are usually associated with the technical side, i.e., the physical. For example, when catching, the message is usually, "Watch the ball", but it lacks the vital psychological component of reminding a player to "Keep your composure and relax".

To perform at your peak, both the physical or technical and the psychological elements must play their part. If necessary, you may focus on one aspect, but don't forget that the other is also important. If too much emphasis is placed on the technical, and not enough on the psychological aspects, our ability to perform is compromised. When both the physical or technical and psychological factors unite, we create the best possible Execution.

Whatever the estimate of how much psychology influences sport, and some research has suggested a figure as high as 80 percent, there are a similar percentage of coaches working on the physical side and on the technical side. This disparity needs to be addressed.

So, let's look at these two major factors in more detail individually, and then analyse how they combine:

1. Physical Execution

On the physical side, Execution is a combination of what is termed the ABCs: Agility, Balance and Coordination, as well as Speed. Each of these needs to be worked on. While all the information here doesn't necessarily pertain only to Execution, this is nevertheless important information for general physical purposes as well as in various guises for the Execution itself.

Agility: This involves changing body position and direction. So, train for these using cones or a ladder, moving through not just laterally, but also instigating a sudden change of direction. My academy teaches this from a young age. One example of these skills can be seen in the picture.

Fitness and fun with the kids

Balance: This involves the ability to control body movement. The use of the core muscles (around the stomach area) is at the heart of balance control.

Two types of balance are static and dynamic. This means Executing from a stationary or a moving position. Thus, you could hit or kick a stationary ball, or a ball on the move. Either way, the control of your balance is important. Practising by shadowing the latter movements or using a balance board would be a great help.

Coordination: This involves the ability to move two or more body parts in a relaxed, flowing and efficient manner. A couple of potential exercises to build coordination are learning to juggle or kicking one ball with your right foot and catching a ball with your left hand and then reversing.

I personally add Core to the equation. There are a plethora of lectures on the Internet to learn about Core. This is the fulcrum of the body, so for success in sport, make sure that you and your teams and pupils work on this.

Speed: This is the ability not only to move quickly, but to sprint off the mark, or to increase the rate of your acceleration. Lying on your back, getting up and sprinting or jumping in the air, or landing with both knees bent are aspects of plyometrics. Loading your thigh muscles and sprinting are guaranteed to improve speed.

Take a Jump

Babe Ruth is one of the great examples of the balance of these four skills. Ruth is generally considered to be one of the greatest baseball players of all time. Not only could he pitch and play in the outfield, but he blew away not only records but the actual physicality of Execution itself.

Ruth changed hitting from a touch and feel skill to one of sheer brute force and power. While pitchers had dominated the game with their throwing skills, Ruth blasted them away with his power. He was the first player to reach homer totals of 30, 40, 50 and even 60.

To achieve this he needed agility, balance, coordination, and speed. I would add to that another point that we will see later, which is the mental side involving confidence, belief, and mental focus.

Muhammad Ali was also a master of speed. With typical humor, he boasted that his speed was such that he could get into bed at night even before the switch had time to turn off the light.

2. Technical Execution

Technical work is the focus of most coaches, i.e., how the body or the object should be moved to create an ideal movement.

The reason the technical part of play is the most popular and easy to work with is because it is explicitly visual. We can see what is happening and that an improvement is being made, or not. Thus, it is easier to analyse, correct or compliment technical and physical shortcomings. Although sports psychology today is a recognised science, the psychological side of sport is still relatively a well of mysterious complexity.

Biles is Miles Apart

No book on sport is complete without the incredible USA gymnast Simone Biles. With thirty titles, she is third on the all-times gymnastics medals list, with numerous golds at both World Championship and Olympic levels.

In my belief, gymnastics is one of the toughest sports in which to achieve extraordinary levels. The demands are so high that, without exceptional physical, tactical, technical, and mental skills, one cannot survive. You can have a bad day at the 'races' or in a match, but the consequences both mentally and physically of a bad day in gymnastics is severe.

Experts talk of Biles's height and strength and weight ratio - she has the perfect match of these in order to perform all the required skills. She has to be agile to twist and flip, bend and extend. Her balance - particularly on the beam, a long piece of wood - has to be perfect. She has the coordination to perform a series of compound and intricate moves all with the unbelievable speed she has at the right time and direction.

I did four years of gymnastics for my physical education training and without doubt, this was the toughest aspect of my course. Besides the variety of apparatuses, the complexity and skills as discussed above were indispensable.

From a RACER perspective there is much for gymnastics to use and lessons for general sportspeople to learn. If I had to single out one RACER element in relation to gymnastics, it would be Execution: the ability to perform both psychological and physical skills.

The aim of this chapter is not to discuss technique per se, but to emphasise its importance in the general scheme of Execution, and that technique is only part of the required understanding and practice. In isolation it is limited and is, in fact, like a smart car with an inadequate engine.

Maverick Geniuses and Making Technical Improvements

There seems to be a range of styles, or biomechanical principles, that are successful with professionals and, indeed, most players of any sport. Of course, there are the mavericks and geniuses that come up with successful results despite their unorthodox techniques. Here are a few stand-out cases:

- Former World No.2 English squash player Peter Marshall played double-handed on both his backhand and forehand. In all my years of playing and teaching the sport, I have never seen anyone play like this, and yet Marshall had perfected this idiosyncrasy to great effect.
- Monica Seles, the former world No.1 ladies tennis champion, also used two hands on both sides. After being stabbed on court in April 1993, she never regained her former level and won only one more Grand Slam title (the ninth of her career) after making her comeback over two years later.

Seles later admitted in her 2009 memoir, *Getting A Grip: On My Body, My Mind, My Self,* that she suffered from depression and a binge eating disorder following the attack. Despite this, Seles' unorthodox style nevertheless cemented her as one of the all-time greats in ladies' tennis.

- One of the greatest football players of all time, Diego Maradona, was also highly unconventional in his style of play. Rather like his younger equivalent, fellow Argentinian Lionel Messi, Maradona rarely used his right foot when striking the ball.

Four minutes after his 'Hand of God' opener early in the second half of the 1986 World Cup quarter-final against England in Mexico City, Maradona ran from inside his own half, took on several players using just his right foot to control the ball, and scored what is still regarded as one of the greatest goals ever seen.

- Peter Reid was one of the England players whom the little genius outran in that brilliant run. Reflecting in his autobiography, *Cheer Up Peter Reid,* he wrote: "From start to finish, the whole run took just under 11 seconds. That was over about 70 yards on an unbearably hot Mexican day and with England's best players doing everything they could to try and stop him in his tracks. As much as I detested what he had done for his first goal, I couldn't help but admire him for his second."

Natural, individual genius is rare. It has usually been guided by brave and visionary coaches who have allowed such talented sports-people to Execute in unusual ways. My advice to pupils who have idiosyncratic styles is to be aware that, percentage wise, it is safer to keep your technique within conventional frameworks.

Each coach or person can – and should – work on the physical Execution as much as necessary, but to re-emphasise, they must remember that it is linked to the psychological aspect of an athlete's make-up.

Honing Specific Execution

The almost unbelievable, phoenix-like return to supremacy of tennis stars Roger Federer and Rafael Nadal in 2017 may largely be attributed to improving the Execution of their backhands.

Both legends would have considered their backhands to be their weaker shot, in contrast to their world No.1 rival, Novak Djokovic, who possesses one of the strongest backhands in the game.

The whole year saw both veterans play more aggressively and positively on the backhand, whereas Djokovic seemed more circumspect. Admittedly, he was hindered by a long-standing elbow injury, but both Federer and Nadal knew they had to improve the Execution of their own backhands if they were to stand any chance against the great Serbian maestro.

Although technique played a vital role, there were other factors, such as choosing to be more aggressive, and having confidence, determination and belief. The psychological side showed its strength for each player, highlighting, in fact, an integrated approach to Execution.

The Psychological Side

Yogi Berra, the great baseball legend, said:

"Ninety percent of the game is half mental."

Basically, psychological Execution is what goes through the mind – or what should be going through the mind – when Executing. What goes through the mind is not as important as what should go through the mind.

Thoughts such as, "I must win this" or "Will I make it?" should be replaced by a state of mind that is not demanding, asking questions or raising doubts. Everyone should, of course, find their own best method. The major aim is to Execute with confidence. This forms the basis of successful Execution.

The psychological side of things is divided into mental and somatic, i.e., the state of our mind and the state of our body. Both need to be in sync for us to perform to our full potential.

Thus, when the elite can't hit a simple putt (the yips) or a kicker misses an easy kick, the mind has become too anxious and the muscles lose their usual control.

Players need to develop mental strategies and techniques to Execute successfully.

Putting the Cart Before the Horse – Performance vs Outcome

One of the most impressive ideas relating to Execution points to the difference between our focus on performance as opposed to looking ahead to a desired outcome. Successful Execution from research is more likely if you concentrate on the former, rather than the latter. Looking ahead creates extra pressure, and affects your Execution, whereas focusing on your immediate Execution results in a more controlled, efficient Execution.

British tennis player Johanna Konta first reached the top 10 in the ladies' world rankings in 2017 and is a great proponent of focusing on performance. She openly states that her focus is what she has the most control over and always takes this pragmatic approach to her game.

"That Ball Was Out!"

Some years ago, I reached a turning point during a tennis match against a tough opponent. I was feeling nervous, struggling to relax and find a rhythm. We were both holding our serve and so decided, as I was losing his serve anyway, that I would try and get some rhythm and not worry about the outcome. I started playing better and then, during a rally, I went for a big winner. It felt and looked great, but it just missed the line and was called out.

To my opponent's surprise, I shouted, "Yes!" He then insisted that the ball had gone out, but I continued to verbally compliment myself. "Yes, yes, yes!" I repeated.

Assuming my positive reaction was tinged with sarcasm, he shouted from across the court: "What is your problem? Your shot was out." I acknowledged that he was quite right, but he still confronted me about why I had acted as if the shot had gone in.

Had I taken this approach every time I missed a shot it would undoubtedly be unsportsmanlike, but this was a one-off occasion and it was at an important point for my personal momentum. The bottom line was that, by focusing on my performance and self-belief, my level improved.

Afterwards, my opponent complained that I had put him off his game. I apologised and insisted that I had not meant to unsettle him, that I had just been struggling with my own demons. I was not prepared to reveal what was, in fact, an incredible breakthrough in my understanding of how to keep my focus in the right direction. My focus was on my performance and this was what led to my desired outcome.

So many mistakes stem from a problem with Choice. If your Choice is made up of one or more elements (for example clarity, visualisation, time, decisiveness), then your mind can be focused solely on the Execution. When the Choice is fuddled so that the full focus isn't on the Execution, then the Execution is compromised. Here is a wonderful story illustrating my points.

One of You Will Die!

This example relates to ultimate focus, from the Zen school of Mahayana Buddhism. Two monks were instructed by their fierce master to compete against each other at chess, warning them that whoever lost would be beheaded. The game went on for hours, with the monks locked in total focus and concentration, with sweat pouring from their bodies.

As the game neared its conclusion, the master appeared with his sword. Steam was now coming off both men as the game was very close. Then, just as the one monk moved his piece to win the game, the master lifted his sword high in the air and exclaimed, "That's what true focus is." Then he walked away.

To focus as if one's life depends on it is an extreme example of concentration and shows what is ultimately possible.

The Mother of Failure

Trying to teach pupils good Execution when they are too nervous or physically tight is tough to accomplish. The aim must be to get the player into a mental state where they can perform unhindered by stress and panic. This may involve utilising breathing control techniques, visualisation and possibly even some fun.

In numerous sports I have taught, when things aren't going well, just changing the verbal environment can make a difference, e.g., start talking about something different but interesting to the player or team. Of course, breaking the stress or tension with a sense of humour also helps.

Primed for Success, Successful in Failure

Yes, this may be a bit rich to say as I am referring to the great New Zealand rugby union team. But how can the greatest team in the history of the sport, the only side to have a winning record against every other nation, only win the World Cup three times (the first in 1987, and then an incredible gap of 24 years to 2011)?

Basically, they somatically froze. They could not get around the mental hurdle at the big moment when they had been favourites for each tournament.

They won again in 2015 and it is clear they worked with specialist psychologists. Besides individual focus, the team were taught to stay in the moment, focus on the performance and not get carried away with outcomes and expectations.

On this subject, numerous people asked me what happened to England, the overwhelming favorite to beat South Africa in the final of the 2019 World Cup in Japan, where I was fortunate enough to watch numerous matches.

The answer is that Eddie Jones overreached on Execution. The England performance in the semifinal against the aforementioned All Blacks was near perfection. So instead of merely praising their performance, he claimed that England could play even better. In effect, they could Execute a perfect game.

This was not necessary. The objective should have been to play their best under the circumstances and not to overreach.

My point was reinforced by Pieter-Steph Du Toit, the South African flanker in the match and World player of the year 2019. He felt he knew they would win within the first ten minutes. England ran the ball from behind their own tryline and several high risk passes, all signs of hubris. He said "I just thought, are you guys crazy? This is a World Cup Final - you don't play like this!"

They got so caught up in this they also underestimated the sheer force, power, and tenacity of the Springboks. Their mindset was so fixed and convinced that their 'perfect' or A game would work, that when it didn't they were shell shocked and could not adjust. It's well known that finals are tense, tough affairs, with both teams giving everything left in them. So in this hubris and possibly inner overconfidence, the whole edifice came crashing down against a brilliant Springbok performance.

Practising the Psychological Under Pressure

I have a great term in my coaching called 'warm-up the score', i.e., practise scoring during physical warm-up before the game starts – and practise under pressure. Anything you can do to put yourself under the upcoming pressure so that, in effect, you have warmed up the score, and pressure moments. So you, say, take a penalty pretending it's the World Cup at stake. Or play a few points and silently score to yourself.

Here is a story to further illustrate my point.

Warming Up the Score

After a warm-up, I passed the ball to my table tennis opponent to start the match and uttered: "8-2" (giving the servers' score first, and thus a 'lead' of six points). He looked at me with surprise and exclaimed: "What?" I caught myself and brushed aside the comment. Then, unbelievably, when I led 8-2 he accused me of mental manipulation.

What had happened was that, while warming up, I had started scoring privately, i.e., 'warming up the score' – and the score was 8-2 to him. Thus, I was losing, which I could have pointed out to him as he was serving – and I did say '8-2'.

The point is that everyone can warm up with no fear of failure and full of confidence. This I have seen at all levels of play in all sports. Then a game starts, and individuals tighten up. This is what happened to my opponent, while I was used to the tension. So, my contention is that people warm up their bodies – but not the score. You can achieve the latter by putting some tension into your warm-up routine through making up a scoreline in your mind. Thus, when the scoring starts in the actual match, you have already gone through the tension of matchplay.

So, a penalty taker in a sport in which penalties are taken should at some point set up a scenario where they say, for example, "This kick to win the match!"

Execution – Bravery and Trust

Fundamentally important for optimum Execution is bravery and trust. After all the physical, tactical and psychological work has been done, what is the most effective way to Execute?

There is much written about trying to get 'into the zone' or 'into the flow', about having the right mindset and honing one's 'inner game' by playing and learning naturally, without being overly self-critical. There are techniques on how to use your breath to relax. Such fine-tuning is aimed at achieving peak performance.

However, while Executing, there is no time for uncertainty and cogitation – there is only time for doing. Anchoring your thought process or using a trigger thought that will help bring you to the right mental state, are useful techniques to utilise immediately prior to Execution.

There comes a point when you must just be brave, trust yourself and rely on your technique. Be courageous, don't let the demons creep in. As the advertising slogan goes, "just do it".

It also reminds me of words in the Leonard Cohen song, *Story of Isaac*, which says not to let a demon or god tempt you. Don't let negative or exciting thoughts distract you. Stay in the moment, stay focused.

Shocked to Hell

I discovered there is a potential third way to achieve the best Execution: SHOCK! For those who have seen the pole vault or tried it, I can assure you that it is one of the most skilful and terrifying sports you can participate in. In my fourth and final year of physical education teacher training it came to the day of our practical pole vault exam. Marks were divided between theory and practical. In relation to the latter, the higher you jumped, the higher your mark.

Now if you consider that we had two 6ft 5ins, 18-19 stone specialist rugby players in our ranks, then you can imagine it was going to be a fun day.

There were nine of us who had survived the four-year course, from an initial intake of 28. As the bar had got higher, people had been forced to drop out. Our practical exam was military-based, and you had to line up army style. When your name was called, you nodded and walked up to the pole and, well, you either attempted the vault into the heavens, or you said, "Pass", and walked silently back to the line.

The start of the runway was very close to where I stood. Knowing I was next, I glanced at my mate, who stood transfixed next to me, his eyes still glazed from his experience: he had called it a day after forcing his way over with a convoluted 'stick-and-hope' leap at three metres.

The bar was now higher, and I nervously picked up the pole. I looked towards the bar and thought, "No way". I then started to try and get the word 'pass' out of my mouth, but to no avail. Then I thought I heard the word coming out. Suddenly, I heard a blood-curdling shout right next to me. My mate had just yelled out straight at me: "Gooooooo!"

I got such a fright that I sprinted with the pole, hit the plinth and found myself hurtling through the air. Fortunately, I felt a soft landing, so I knew I was safe. Then I heard probably the most raucous laughter in my life. I had done it – from sheer fright.

Our lecturer said that he had known the external examiner for 15 years and that this was the first time he had ever seen him actually laugh. The event was the foundation of my idea on bravery and trust. I call it my 'pole vault idea'. Internally, you just have to shout to yourself: 'GO!'

Counting To 10

Getting the best amount of tension into your play is vital for Executing. A great phrase to remember is the difference between being intense and tense. If '1' is too relaxed and '10' too tense, by playing on a number somewhere in between these it will help you find the right intention in your play. You can use extremes, e.g. '2' and '8', then you will notice the difference when you try '4'. So, you play over-relaxed, i.e., '2', then over-tense to '8', squeezing hands and muscles as appropriate. This works and is really a great way to access your best intensity level.

Execution Support

Situations in which we may not be Executing but which are still integral to the action may be called Execution Support. So, while you may not be Executing as such, you make a choice to Execute movement. For example, an attacking player in a field sport might Execute a forward run in Anticipation of a through-ball. Or a doubles tennis player might Execute a move away from the net to the baseline to support their defending partner.

How Very Rude

Once, in a difficult mixed doubles tennis match, my partner and I were playing in a third and deciding final set. My partner, despite some great ground shots, had been unable to hold her serve once. Her serve was weak, and the returners' very good. I decided to act fast for her next service game.

Point 1 – I faded into the middle, opening the tramlines of the court to create indecision. The male opponent took the bait, panicked and duly pushed the ball out wide: 15-0.

Point 2 – I repeated the trick, and the female opponent took the bait. Seeing me move left, she tightened up, and the ball hit the net: 30-0.

Point 3 – A fast serve down the middle, which was close to the tramlines and tough to return, so I squeezed the middle of the court and the male opponent went too wide with his shot: 40-0.

Point 4 – We played the 'I formation', i.e., with me starting in the middle, forcing the opponent to guess which way I was going to return. The applied pressure forced her to tighten, she didn't select her shot clearly and cracked, with the ball going out. Game over.

As we walked to change ends, the male opponent turned to me and praised me for a great game. My partner, in response to me, commented: "Is he being funny? You didn't even touch the ball!"

In a nutshell, there were four Execution Supports, zero touches of the ball, one vital game won.

Execution Success – Be A Winner

Let's look at some factors in Execution Success:

- Having a degree of technical proficiency.
- Making good Choices.
- Being able to Execute the Choice you made. Be decisive.
- Being tough under pressure, whether from the score or from opponents.

- Concentrating focus on what you are doing. There is a phase from accessing concentration to Execution concentration.
- Dealing with environmental factors, such as weather, people or crowds.
- Dealing with personal stress. Use this to your advantage. Become more determined with the job at hand.

In Summary

After all the pre-Execution work, it's the Execution that defines our success. Enjoyment, hopefully, is always there. I can honestly say that although it hurt to lose matches, some of my – and my teams' – losses were Execution at its best and sport at its most thrilling, but the opponent was just too good.

In this chapter, I have tried to show the different types and skills involved in Execution. One needs nerves of steel and self-belief. Learn to solve problems as each situation brings up new challenges. In fact, sport could partly be defined as a problem-solving activity.

In addition, I have shown there are two components of Execution, i.e., the physical and the psychological. While we can work on them separately or combined, in actual play they are one. Historically, the latter has been given less attention and I am adding to the importance of this area. While many theories and systems abound, it's up to the coach or individual to integrate psychological forms or methods into their Executions.

I have tried to offer just some of the many ideas out there to help players Execute much more confidently and better. But we must also remember to enjoy ourselves, to admire the beauty and thrill of the sport and the chase to ignite positive stress, the adrenaline coursing through you. This may seem obvious but I myself, and from many other players' stories, realise we can sometimes get caught up in the cut and thrust and 'winning is everything' mentality with a possible loss of perspective.

But don't go away – we are not finished! Execution is only part of the RACER flow and there is one final component to go.

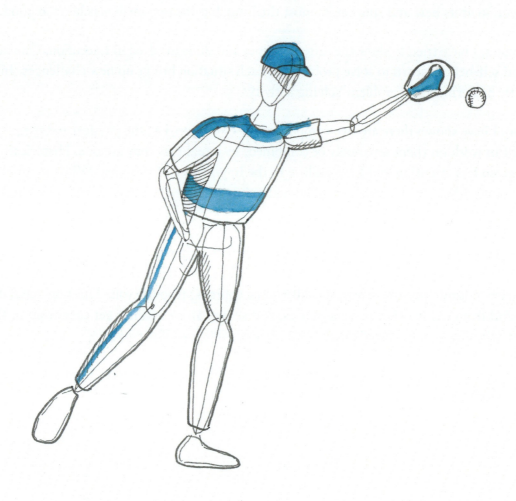

Chapter 5

RECOVERY

"It's hard to beat a person who never gives up."

- BABE RUTH

The last letter in the RACER acronym, 'R', involves our skills and ability to Recover in order to be Ready again. People making the comment "recovery is obvious" may be surprised, as I elaborate on elite performers, examining and analysing different, deeper aspects and techniques, leading to what I term radical Recovery.

You shouldn't just Execute and watch. Part of the skill of Execution is the ability to Recover. As an example, it's usually not enough to merely kick, pass or hit and see what happens. Part of your movement after doing this is your ability to psychologically and physically Recover. At all levels in sport, including at the elite level, I see "watching Execution", i.e., observing your own Execution, on a regular basis. To keep the successful flow of the RACER system, you must "radically Recover". This requires a combination of tactical, physical, psychological and technical skills.

Each sport has its own Recovery situations and skills with which to return to the optimum Ready state. However, there are similarities and essential fundamentals in whichever sport you play. Whatever the action, the bottom line is, radically Recover, as effectively and as fast as you can, to be dynamically Ready and take on the next part of the action.

Recovery that is consistently performed requires the highest concentration, both mentally and physically. As the body and mind begin to tire, the ability to Recover becomes tougher.

When talking about effective Recovery, it is helpful to remember the cyclical nature of the RACER system.

The RACER Cycle:

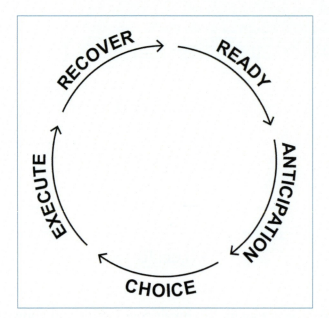

The better your Recovery, the more effectively you will transition back into Ready, and the more likely the success of the next phase of action, whether you are directly involved or not. In other words, whether you have Executed, or watched your team-mate or the opponent Execute, you still need to Recover to the best position that is tactically possible.

Let's look at a map of Recovery. Coaches and players can use this as a basis and explore, using their own knowledge and information in this chapter, to understand and then practically train and perform as suggested.

The Five Major Divisions of Recovery:

- Set breaks
- Breaks in play
- During the action
- Post-action
- Post-match or practise

While I will comment on each aspect, the overall area that I want to focus on is Recovery after Execution.

Set Breaks

These are official breaks of play, for example, after a quarter or at half-time in American football or basketball, a change of ends in table tennis or tennis, an end of innings in cricket or baseball, or a drinks break.

These breaks are great Recovery moments. Football managerial legend Sir Alex Ferguson was renowned for his 'hair dryer' team-talks during which the Manchester United players were told exactly what they had done badly, and what they needed to do to right those wrongs. By the time they returned to the action they had Recovered, Ready for the second half.

It was during a scheduled break during the US Open men's final of 2012 that the British tennis legend, Andy Murray, found the mental resolve to change his life.

Having squandered a two-set lead against Novak Djokovic, Murray went for a toilet break ahead of the fifth and deciding set, in the knowledge that he was facing his fourth defeat in a Grand Slam. He later recalled looking into the changing room mirror and asking himself, "How much do you really want this?"

Having conquered his demons, Murray went back on court with his mental and physical Readiness restored. He went on to break Djokovic in the first game of the final set and had no trouble closing out the final 6-2 to win his first Grand Slam title.

Breaks in Play

A break in play is an opportunity to psychologically and physically Recover. At this point the captain can take the chance to talk to the players, or the players can refocus themselves.

During the Action

The bread and butter work of Recovery is performed on a time spectrum which varies between – and within – each sport. There are instantaneous moments to Recover, and times when there is an appropriate time to do this. My suggestion is to work on not just the most important, but on a variety of Recovery situations.

Take American football. There are many situations and types of Recovery in this sport. Often, the attacking, defensive or kicking team is off the field and this is static Recovery time. While on the field, each person and position has their specific non-attacking Recovery role.

In tennis, you may be volleying and have little time to react, or players may have a slow rally and you then have – or can – create more Recovery time. The faster the play, the closer you are to the net and the faster your Recovery needs to be.

Flat-Footed Recovery

I have often noticed during training that people are so caught up with completing the Execution and its subsequent results that the mental, tactical and physical switch to Recovery doesn't happen as efficiently as it should.

The following three examples from tennis, football and cricket show that Recovery during play often needs more concerted practice. They may also help to illustrate the attention and commitment to detail that good Recovery requires. Without it, we are often caught flat-footed, which can cost a game.

Example 1 - The Talented Server in Tennis

If you go to a court and watch people practising their serve, I can almost certainly guarantee most players will not be practising their Recovery after serving. It's much more fun just to serve repeatedly and only look to see if the ball went in or to concentrate on where you were aiming, while neglecting to practise Recovery after each serve. It takes conscious effort and discipline to hit a serve and Recover in practise. I know this for myself.

The second shot after your serve is one of the most difficult to play, because the pressure of serving and the quick action of the serve requires an immediate readjustment of your body. After serving, the rhythm of your next shot can easily be put out of kilter. Added to this, the usually fast pace of the serve means the return comes back even faster, making a full Recovery for the next shot harder, but even more essential.

When I ask people to practise their Recovery after the serve, I'm often surprised at how difficult many people find it and, generally, how poorly it is performed. Yet this aspect is probably one of, if not *the* most important areas of the game.

When Recovery Is Ignored

At a mundane on-court tennis lecture one day, my sight drifted to a very good performance. A talented boy of around 15 years old was practising his serve, but not once in the 20 minutes of working with his coach did he practise his Recovery after hitting the ball. His footwork after serving was sloppy, and he only seemed concerned with how well he had executed his last serve. I wondered how he would perform in a match situation.

A short while later, another very good player turned up for a practice match against the teenager. My suspicion was verified. His Recovery after serving was poor and he missed an unnecessary number of second shots. His coach kept on correcting his stroke-play, but not the crucial cause of the error: his poor Recovery.

Example 2 - The Great Pretenders in Football

When players are running in their attempt to score or defend, how many of them really try at full Recovery after that phase of play is over? While it's true that the better and fitter teams and players do this more frequently, it's also the case that just one small error in not Recovering can be disastrous at the more competitive levels.

I have often seen what I call 'pretend recovery': players making half-hearted attempts, hoping a goal is scored, or not. Look out for it when a goal is scored and see which players are fully committed to returning to their best possible tactically Ready position. Who is Recovering the best and who is possibly not going to be dynamically Ready for the next action?

Example 3 - Neglect at Your Peril in Cricket

If you watch a team practising in the nets, you'll see most bowlers working hard to get the batsman out, but not making too much effort to catch or stop a ball that is struck towards them. Fielding is not their main objective during a training session.

But I maintain that in the modern game, and particularly in the limited overs formats, every run can be crucial, so bowlers should also work on their Recovery after each delivery. From a more dynamically Ready position, they can work on both fielding and reflex catching.

Practising this more in training could prove to be pivotal in a competitive match, and yet I've rarely seen match-intensity Recovery from a bowler during a cricket training session.

Recovery: A Perspective on Time

Recovery is divided into different time and speed dimensions or frames. To explain this more clearly, you can create a time spectrum from 1-10, with '1' being the shortest amount of time possible to Recover, and '10' being the longest. Thus, a fast bowler trying to return-catch a hard-hitting batsman could be rated as a '1'. Likewise, a boxer needs to be quick to Recover from a swinging opponent. During a field sports match, the Recovery time is often not urgent. This is because the ball moves around the field and you have time to move around, though this of course varies. As your involvement and the situation develops, you may need exceptionally fast Recovery skills.

For example, when a goalkeeper blocks a shot, they then need to get up, ie., Recover, very fast. Or someone gets past you and you need to Recover to get back at them.

Basketball is a court game which involves very fast Recovery. On attack, the player needs to Recover to possibly receive the ball, or Recover into a good defensive Ready position. This is also an example not only of time in Recovery, but all-round Recovery as opposed to golf, which requires more of a mental Recovery. In this very different sport, '10' might be a golfer who has plenty of time to Recover before he plays his next stroke. Though, as mentioned, most sports have a range and mix of Recovery times on this response spectrum.

What is important is for each coach and player to look at all the relevant areas, and work both on the slower reflex Recovery skills as well as the faster ones.

I used to play hockey for my teaching college and remember one competition in which the standard was low, giving me time to basically run the show! Two hours later, I was on the field in a National First Division match and for the first 20 minutes I was outplayed, out-run and brushed aside.

The coach called me off to see if I wanted to be subbed but I reassured him that I would be fine. The fact was, the game at that level was far quicker than the college competition I had been playing only a little while earlier, and I was struggling to transfer to a mode of lightning-fast Recovery. This affected my Ready position and the performance then spiraled down from there. Once my Recovery and reflexes improved, I was back to normal and went on to play a satisfying game.

The Four Major Types of Recovery

During action, four very important Recovery skills and levels of knowledge need to be developed:

- Physical Recovery
- Tactical Recovery
- Psychological Recovery
- Technical Recovery

If all four of these are appropriately applied, then the efficiency and efficacy of radical Recovery is assured.

As mentioned before, the psychological aspect is not obvious to the untrained eye, and it is usually given the least attention. For example, "Come on, move!" (physical Recovery) and "Where are you running to?" (tactical Recovery) are often heard, whereas, "Where's your head?" or "Forget about the last play, get Ready" (psychological Recovery) are less prevalent.

It's vital to remember that the psychological aspect of Recovery, clearing the mind of stress or clutter, should be worked on.

1. Physical Recovery

Sometimes in my physical Recovery I feel at my most dynamic, especially under pressure. I feel my thighs and my arms pumping, my heart beating and the adrenaline furious, my centre of gravity low as I fly back to position or chase the next ball or person. I don't like not being able to get to any ball, or letting a person pass me. I never forget the words of the tenacious US tennis legend, Jimmy Connors:

"Chase the impossible you may even get to some."

In the picture here, you can see me feeling the same as Connors: full of energy, my weight leaning towards where I am Recovering to, and about to explode back to position. This physical Recovery style of correct weight and balance distribution is applicable to all sports.

Mike's weight on inside foot for efficient recovery

My academy even has an exercise in Connor's honour, called 'Impossible'. The feeds are so difficult it's almost impossible to get balls back. But occasionally someone does, and the kids go crazy with mutual joy that one of their fellows has broken the coach's claim of 'Impossible'. When our youngsters play matches, they are brilliant at getting tough balls back because of this drill.

Back from the Dead

Some players are simply spectacular when it comes to physical Recovery. A perfect example is from the Rome Masters tennis final between Andy Murray and Novak Djokovic in May 2016.

Defending champion Djokovic was losing 3-6, 3-5, and facing match point at 15-40 down. Despite being forced to deliver a second serve, Djokovic was controlling the point. The pressure was all on Murray who was running, stretching and fighting to keep his match point alive. The Serb played a near unreturnable shot, deep to the Scot's backhand, pushing him wide. Somehow, Murray managed to return, but he was only able to give Djokovic an 'easy' high backhand at the net.

To the amazement of the crowd, not only did Murray somehow Recover but, as he split-stepped he anticipated Djokovic's next shot and thrashed a winner down the line on the run, deep into the open court

I doubt there have been many better Recovery and finish shots on match point in the history of the sport. Murray defeated the defending champion to lift the title for the first time.

Parents Know Best

I once ran an Under-12s football team and one day the parents turned up towards the end of a training session to see their kids lying flat on the grass. One of the mothers was surprised and curious and asked what was going on. "Just watch," I smiled.

Suddenly, I shouted: "Go!"

The players shot up off the ground. "Down" I shouted, and they were on the deck in a flash. I repeated this exercise a few times. It was great to watch their enthusiasm and speed off the mark. "Not vertical too quick", or "use your arms" were incidentally some of the technical Recovery aspects. But essentially this is about Recovering off the floor but also a good exercise to strengthen the muscles for physical Recovery.

A huge round of applause broke out as the sweating and proud players completed the exercise.

---

2. Tactical Recovery

Good tactical Recovery is the ability to Recover to the best possible position, so you are Ready to respond for your next action. This does require knowledge and understanding of your sport. As Aristotle noted, 'To know the good is to do the good'.

Great players always Recover to the best possible tactical position for themselves or the team. When you see players at the very highest level not always making good tactical Recovery decisions, it points to the very strong possibility that less skilled players also fail to do so – only worse.

Tactical Recovery requires Anticipation because without understanding what may occur, you wouldn't know where to Recover to. I give three examples here to illustrate that positioning is integral to sound tactical Recovery.

Example 1: Rugby – In rugby union, if you are attacking and you have a chance to win the game with a try or a drop goal, the fly-half, who is one of the players most likely to get the ball, must decide on his tactical Recovery.

During overtime in the 2018 Six Nations clash between France and Ireland, Irish fly-half Johnny Sexton had to decide whether to Recover to the right or left of the ruck, and how far back his Recovery position should be. With one last chance to snatch victory from the jaws of defeat, Sexton dropped further back than usual. The rest, as they say, is history.

Sexton's immaculate long-range drop goal secured a 15-13 victory on the way to Ireland's third Grand Slam. Sexton's positioning was an Anticipated, tactical Recovery which enabled his country to secure the last-gasp victory.

Example 2: Football – When a defender is running backwards, he must see which attacker, if any, is running behind him to mark or track his opponent's movements. And yet, week after week, I see players aimlessly running back and displaying a hopeful Recovery, rather than making an astute tactical Recovery, getting closer to the opponent to make sure it's tougher or impossible to score. Do this, rather than watch a flying shot scorch into the net and look surprised.

Example 3: Tennis – I recall a tennis match where I was in danger of losing heavily. I was under pressure and Recovering to just behind the baseline, but it was making little difference to my game as I was still being rushed and outplayed. So, I changed my Recovery position to further back behind the baseline to give myself more time to return his shot. The difference in my fortunes was immediate. After the match my opponent said, "Wow, you really picked up your level of play!" But it wasn't my improved play that was the catalyst to my comeback. It was my tactical Recovery position that made the difference.

3. Psychological Recovery

"My body could stand the crutches, but my mind couldn't stand the sideline."

– Michael Jordan

The power of psychological Recovery is immense and, as I noted earlier, often underestimated. As the stabilising force behind all sport, I see psychological Recovery as the foundation of Recovery.

After any action in sport, getting your mind back to the optimum state of being Ready requires several skills. Foremost is focusing on what's next, and not getting unnecessarily caught up in positive or negative actions, e.g., being overconfident or losing confidence. This all-important awareness of knowing what you need to do must be conscientiously ingrained for it to become part of unconscious competence in Recovery.

*Taking full advantage of breaks in play to refocus our energies and recover our
mental and physical strength is essential to improving our game.*

Tennis specialist Steve Goepel examined the fact that there is more time spent between points than in real play, raising the vital issue of what is, and what is not, done mentally during these 'non-action' periods of Recovery time.

Similarly, in football, how much time during the 90 minutes (plus stoppages) is the ball in play, and how well do players utilise this time to Recover to their optimum Ready state?

In late November 2017, football statisticians OPTA released data concerning English Premier League clubs which suggested that the ball was in play during West Ham United home matches (by that stage of the season) for just 53 minutes, 34 seconds. Noted as the worst culprits, the 'best' was just shy of five minutes longer – at Chelsea's Stamford Bridge. Such Recovery time can be used to plan tactics and strategies, Recover physically and to centre players emotionally.

Mental Clarity

The mind in sport is like a sealed jar of crystal-clear water with orange sand at the bottom. Once play starts, the sand is disturbed and begins to fill with random particles which begins to discolour the water. The harder the match situation, the more disparate the sand becomes and the cloudier the water.

The aim of Recovery is that after each action of play we must keep the water as clear as possible. The better you Recover, the clearer the water (the mind) will be to return to being properly Ready. It may be tough to fully return the water to its original clarity, but the better the player Recovers psychologically, the more likely they are to achieve a dynamically Ready state for the next phase of action.

A classic example of psychological Recovery springs to mind. In February 2018, Liverpool and Tottenham Hotspur played an enthralling Premier League match in which Spurs striker Harry Kane missed a crucial penalty which threatened to cost them the game. Then, with just a few seconds left, the Londoners were awarded another spot-kick. Kane now had the high-pressure responsibility of saving the game himself or offering the opportunity – and subsequent pressure – to a team-mate. Kane decided to take the penalty and scored confidently, ensuring a point from the 2-2 draw. His ability to Recover psychologically, to stay confident and focused after a potentially disastrous missed penalty was remarkable. It takes great mental discipline and dedication to attain this level of clarity.

4. Technical Recovery

This involves the best way to Recover using the body in the best biomechanical way, with an awareness of where your physical Recovery requires improvements.

On this point, many years ago at a tennis conference in the USA, a biomechanics coach discussed Andy Roddick, a former world No.1, and his Recovery weakness from the backhand side of the court. Basically, it turned out that the technical use of his left foot was not as good as his right because it turned out to be weaker. The result was, after hard work, this fault was rectified.

Note in the picture how I am using the crossover step. My left foot is crossing over the right and is the fastest way to get back to position without turning and running. It requires technical strength and dynamic balance and was the aspect I just mentioned that Roddick was working on.

Mike using crossover step

Some technical issues involve sidestepping or crossover steps.

The latter are quicker to perform, but before finishing Recovery you need the flexibility of movement and stability of the sidestep.

How do you break when running fast so you can Recover? One of the moves in tennis is the triangle step, where you bring your back foot round to the outside acting as a break, while your body weight goes towards the inside, so you can move back to position.

Another Recovery situation is getting off the floor in various sports. The way you push off matters, keeping your centre of gravity low, so you can technically push off with more power and use your hands to drive your body.

In Summary

I have shown that there is more to work on concerning Recovery than initially meets the eye. This means that writing down all areas of Recovery that are relevant in your sport, possibly in groups (e.g. set plays, starts or attacking situations) or order of priority, will assist your efforts.

To work on Recovery, it is useful to have a map that shows the territory from which we can see where we should be working, or what areas we should be examining.

We see that there are time elements involved in Execution to Recovery, as well as aspects in which we have considered Recovery time such as natural game intervals, e.g., a corner.

To have complete Recovery we must consider the four major determiners: physical, tactical, psychological and technical. I'd like to summarise this with a relevant example from cricket that exemplifies all areas.

Recovery Creates Cricketing History

In the 1981 Ashes Test at Headingley, to all intents and purposes England were down and out. Angus Fraser, reflecting on the series in *The Independent* described the outcome in the following words:

> *'It was a turnaround so implausible it still beggars belief; a spectacular resurrection in one man's career, in the fortunes of a team and in the morale of a nation."*

After the first innings, the home side were 174 runs behind Australia, who forced the follow-on. In the second innings, they collapsed again, and at 135-7 were still 39 runs behind. There seemed very little or no chance of victory, which led to most of the England players checking out of their hotel, expecting to be home that night.

Then Ian Botham, who had resigned as captain and who was not in a great space mentally, having made a pair in the previous match, which had been drawn at Lord's, cut loose. Joined at the crease by his good friend, Graham Dilley, Botham is reputed to have said: "Right then, let's have a bit of fun."

He duly smashed an incredible 149no. Dilly, more renowned as a bowler, made 56. England in the end had set Australia a very standard 124 to win and were at one stage looking comfortable at 56-1. Then Bob Willis took over and took eight wickets for 43 runs to pull off an astonishing victory.

To win, England needed Recovery in every area discussed. They achieved this to record one of the greatest Test cricket and sporting comebacks of all time.

Botham and Dilley Recovered from the jaws of defeat and despair to a state of relaxed and spontaneous Readiness. The Australians probably didn't Recover and weren't as Ready to perform as they should have been. Two of their players even bet against them losing when the odds of 500-1 were too tempting not to take.

Then, when bowling, England Recovered their fight, believing they had a chance and with pride at stake. The captain, Mike Brearley, set a good tactical field. England fielded incredibly well as Willis Recovered his fire and his tactical, technical and psychological ability to bowl like a man possessed. In fact, in the first innings he failed to take a wicket from his 30 overs.

So, while there are many elements to this story, there is no disputing that this is an incredible achievement of Recovery.

Now you have read through the five elements of RACER, it may be time to give yourself a deserved Recovery or review time. Once you have done this, I am sure you will enjoy reading about SELF, which I really consider to be essential for any good coach, and a very interesting template to anyone in a pedagogic role.

Chapter 6

SELF

"Some people say I have attitude – maybe I do… but I think you have to. You have to believe in yourself when no one else does – that makes you a winner right there."

– VENUS WILLIAMS

'Know thyself' is an aphorism from the famous oracle at the Temple of Apollo in Delphi, Greece. In ancient Greece, people came from far and wide to ask the oracle for answers to the riddles and mysteries in their lives.

The oracle's wise advice, to know oneself, seems to me to be one of the core principles in life. Indeed, a March 2019 article in *The Guardian* by Hadley Freeman resonated, proffering the advice to teenage girls that, "I really recommend getting to know yourself before your mid-30s." Similarly, in both the context of coaching not only for the coach as a person, but in your relationship with your players and team members, I suggest you 'know yourSELF'.

Psychologist Michael Gervais has many years of experience working with professional sportspeople. Working with elite sportspeople, he has looked at the common thread of how the greatest performers in the world use their minds to pursue the boundaries of their potential.

Greaves knows that without a firm base and grasp of the SELF, it's very hard to anchor oneSELF on the path to success. He believes that to achieve what I would call a fulfilled SELF, in the personal use of the word, and to have success in sport, it is essential that you must know:

- What your personal philosophy is
- What you stand for
- What your guiding principles are

In addition, you must be able to articulate these principles even under extreme pressure. You must be clear about the vision you have for the future and how you want to experience your future.

He talks about how we treat our SELF when things are bad, or going well, and to discover these behaviours within ourselves. He explains the skills you need to talk about yourself when you are great. What are the environmental factors that affect how we deal with a situation that's negative?

I developed the acronym SELF after many years of thinking deeply about what constitutes the core principles of coaching. With many great words, four stuck out as essential. These words, or in fact principles, are: Safety, Enthusiasm, Learning, and Fun - so the acronym SELF. I have included the acronym in this book because I feel it is so important. If coaches or teachers are using RACER with their students, then this should be passed on through the rounded pedagogic psychology of SELF. Once I was satisfied with the efficacy of SELF as a concept, I began presenting it, including it within the academy, writing papers on it, and offering insights to coaches.

An article I wrote in the *British Tennis Coaches Association* magazine was very well received. Many coaches contacted me remarking on the productive effect this had on their coaching relationships. In fact, anyone coaching under my wing is required to understand and practice these principles.

One of my further revelations was to apply this principle to the relationship with oneself. Do unto your SELF as you want others to do to you. I will expand on this idea later in this chapter.

How do we improve ourselves as sports enthusiasts and as coaches? Does a goal, a target, a template or some analytical system help? The answer to all of these is a most definite 'yes'.

Books, courses and articles abound in this area, and most views and evidence point to the benefits of having guides to help us get where we want to be. Such guides could be a set goal, an action plan, a template or an acronym.

In this case, SELF is the template and provides the ideal acronym to encapsulate and relay, in a balanced and sensible way, our relationship commitments. I am very excited and proud of this acronym and feedback has been tremendous.

At its most essential level, SELF reminds us that we learn best
in a Safe environment from an Enthusiastic teacher
who makes the Learning clear, relevant and Fun.

The SELF Diamond:

SELF covers a broad spectrum of human interaction. Combined and used authentically, the four elements form a very powerful dynamic. Over the years, I have come to see that understanding and practicing SELF is fundamental to successful coaching.

It is important to stress that these four elements are not isolated concepts. While they can function relatively independently, they are essentially integrated.

Coaches Getting Sacked

In the football world, managers get dismissed from their roles far too easily. The ostensible reason is poor results. Is this the only reason? Why did poor results occur? A likely reason is a weakness with SELF, regarding coach and players. Here are some scenarios:

- The players no longer feel emotionally safe.
- Players are subject to private or public humiliations.
- The enthusiasm of the coach is replaced with anger, over-control and a sour demeanour as results go against the team.
- Learning is repetitive, failing to produce positive results, so that development and growth is stymied.
- The sessions aren't enjoyable and become a chore.

There just needs to be enough dissatisfaction to tip the players as a group against the coach and it is job over.

In the rest of this chapter, we will look more closely at Safety, Enthusiasm, Learning and Fun in turn.

1. Safety

Safety is an ongoing, dynamic process of awareness, assessment and implementation. It's not just a list of personal welfare and well-being checks which coaches normally abide by. Pupils must feel safe in all respects. From the moment they arrive, until after they have left a session, it is imperative that pupils feel emotionally, psychologically and physically safe.

After dominating cycling at the 2012 and 2016 Olympics, the win-at-all-cost attitude of the Great Britain team, which seemingly disregarded certain cyclists' emotional safety, became public knowledge. Intimidation, bullying, sexism and crudeness were evidently endemic within the cycling organisation and several athletes complained about not feeling safe. This approach was unsustainable, compromising the performers' psychological safety.

A tricky dilemma to assess is: when is too much, *too* much? At what cost is a medal or a victory earned? Each situation should be discussed independently, but all I can suggest is that safety, in its all-encompassing sense, is paramount to any coaching success. Although you may work in a group, people are individuals who, when possible, need to be treated as such. The saying of 'one-size-doesn't-fit-all' is very appropriate to safety.

On a physical safety level, I am fastidious. I allow no ball on or near the playing area and, in fact, have taken pictures and been shocked to watch renowned coaches at high-level training events disregarding this principle.

A prime example of this was when Australia bowler Glenn McGrath slipped on a ball during the warm-up on the morning of the second Ashes Test at Edgbaston in 2005. Ruled out by an ankle ligament injury, many believe his absence (he had taken nine wickets in his side's 239-run victory in the first Test at Lord's) was a key factor in England's subsequent triumph.

How to Rearrange Your Face!

Any of my pupils, past or present, might recognise my, on occasion, sarcastic introduction to highlighting the importance of safety. Such as how to get your teeth knocked out, your lip cut, your head busted open or even a smack in the groin!

In my lessons, I demonstrate how best to achieve these results. If the group and I gel, and it's the right time and place, it can be hilarious and very effective. So, for example, delivering a warning about the danger of getting your teeth knocked out is best achieved on the backswing of someone serving. At this point it is important to walk past them when they are swinging their racket back – and you must make sure you are smiling. The head whack, in my experience, is best achieved when taking a shortcut past someone swinging a forehand and getting too close to them.

I warn both parties to be aware and fortunately, as I compile the academy's safety record, it is as near to perfect as I would want.

Safe Banter – Goad or Own Goal

One common way of eliciting humour in teaching is through light-hearted teasing. The problem is that everyone might laugh, including the person being teased, but this is what I would call 'fake fun'. Emotionally, the person being teased may be negatively affected and, in my experience, often feels humiliated. Banter at the right time can be beneficial, but beware of the risk to a player's emotional safety.

At the highest level, all the slagging and slandering from players, opposing fans and the press requires psychological resilience. I am not a fanatically politically correct coach because it is essential for pupils and players to build up some resilience against the incessant barrage of 'psychological warfare'. Players must learn to roll with the punches and not overreact to teasing and goading.

This is in no way condoning such behaviour. We live in a more educated and aware world and there is no excuse for homophobic, racist or other such offensive behaviour and I certainly don't tolerate it. I have been on the receiving end of this abuse once at 4-0 up in the final set of a tennis match as my opponent did everything he could to unnerve me. But I saw his ploy and was able to focus on the task at hand. And no, I did not shake his hand at the end.

Success Is Not Safety

While it is very difficult to judge from the outside and without knowing the details, it seems that success in many sports does not equate to safety. The demands, the intensity, the cut-throat nature of sport can lead to players, parents, and coaches to abuse individuals' safety. Not to mention, of course, drug taking and cheating.

2. Enthusiasm

To be taught by someone who shows passion and enthusiasm for their sport and coaching makes a big difference to enjoyment and success levels. Even the highest performing and best-paid sports-people thrive on positive, enthusiastic coaches. I often read about players whose success or failure is strongly influenced by the respective coach. An example is German footballer Mezut Ozil: rich, famous, talented, a World Cup winner, needing 'an arm around the shoulder' from his then coach at Arsenal, Arsene Wenger. Or 2019 Australian Open tennis champion Naomi Osaka falling out with her coach who, for whatever reason, was hardly saying a word to her.

One classic comment came from a 14-year-old:

"It must be hard being a coach with the personality of a cardboard box."

Even at this relatively young age, the boy had correctly recognised the importance of a coach possessing an enthusiastic and energetic personality.

The skill of the voice is essential. It is key to effective communication, as well as for stimulating motivation. Using the appropriate inflections in tone, at the right time, and with honest intent and care, demonstrates an effective and enthusiastic coach. Enthusiasm, correctly projected, is infectious – it rubs off on everyone involved.

Passion and Positive Body Language

Writing in *The Daily Telegraph* in 2017, Alan Tyers asked the veteran boxing and athletics BBC commentator, Mike Costello, for some top broadcasting tips. The first one he highlighted was enthusiasm.

"Above all, you need passion. If you are not feeling and showing that, you can't expect your audience to feel it."

The same attitude applies to coaching. When giving positive encouragement and constructive criticism, the key is in finding the right balance and timing with the way you speak and use language. Too much praise can lose its effect, while too much criticism can have a negative impact. Enthusiasm shows you care, that you want something positive for your players. This affects learning, energy levels and enjoyment.

Facial and body language are also very important when conveying your enthusiasm. People pick up on negative body language when they are tired and things aren't going well. Thus, it is important to be aware of, and practise, how you present yourself publicly.

Whatever thought or action you undertake, you need to keep or reboot the enthusiasm. It doesn't mean being manic, but rather keeping an energy level conducive to providing a positive effect.

Playing the Part

One point made by the late, fantastic Canadian tennis coach, Peter Burwash, has stayed with me. Burwash noted how the coach is like an actor. Whatever the sport, you must play a role that helps get the best out of your pupils or players.

Portray yourself as the best, most professional and enthusiastic coach. Get into your acting role. This is not being false, but it's a very clever way to psychologically achieve enthusiasm and confidence. I make this point to many an aspiring coach, as well as to people asking me for coaching tips.

Like most people, I have had tough and difficult moments in my life and career. Yet I am very proud to say that very rarely have pupils asked me if there was a problem, and this has a lot to do with my commitment to always showing enthusiasm.

I have discovered that enthusiasm is an art which can only be improved over time. You become your own personal conductor, producing a performance to the benefit of all those you are responsible for.

By the same token, I confess to being prone to teaching too much. My enthusiasm and fervent desire to improve my pupils' performance has led in the past to giving not only too much information but trying to do too much work on too many skills. As one of my social-level pupils said sarcastically to me: "Mike, I don't need to get to play Wimbledon this year!"

Finding the right balance between enthusiasm and overkill is a crucial factor in our coaching endeavours.

The Bad Boy Bunks School

My father was the social manager for the 1970 touring Australian cricket team in South Africa and I, to the great envy of my friends, was invited to join in with some of the cricketers, partly based on my enthusiasm.

I had overheard my father talking to the Australian manager about when and where practise was to be held. My problem was that the session would end before I finished school for the day. I figured if I could leave school a couple of hours early, I'd be able to take a bus and catch some of the session. So, to the horror of my friends, I just walked out of school through a concealed gap in the boundary fence.

Wow, what a thrill! My fear was increased by the possibility of my father being there, but I banked on him being at work and crept into the practice area. For an hour, I stood right by the side of the nets while my heroes from the opposition practised. As I was in school uniform, one of the coaches asked if I should be in class.

I responded: "No, I am not meant to be, but don't tell my dad!" The Aussies cracked up laughing.

Retrieving a ball or being asked to throw a few at a famous batsman before he went into the nets, was pure sports heaven. No punishment from school or parents could dampen that experience. At the tender age of 16, I was already a committed fan and player of all available sports. Throughout my career, I have managed to keep this unbridled passion and enthusiasm alive. It hasn't waned with age and remains a keystone to my coaching success.

3. Learning

Quality and constructive teaching is exhilarating. It helps motivate, inspire and bring the best out of you and your team. Most people want to improve in the sport they play. The onus then is on the coach to try and facilitate learning in training, a match or a team-talk.

In addition, it is important to motivate players as well as reinforce learning. For consistency of delivery and to show parents what the pupils have learnt, we hand out learning cards. Pupils put stickers on both sides of the card when they have covered that aspect. The front is the RACER system and the back covers the fundamentals of every sport. This even includes sportsmanship. Rewards are then given halfway through and on completion of the card.

Camp Card front

Camp Card back

> ### What Did We Learn?
>
> One summer day, a mother called me after her children had returned home from one of my tennis camps to say that her kids had really enjoyed themselves. But when she asked them what they had learnt they responded that they had just had lots of fun and games.
>
> I asked her to look at their camp learning cards. Sure enough, she found them in their lunchboxes, brought the cards to the phone and commented on several of the stickers on the cards. I confirmed that what was noted was what they had learnt that day.
>
> "Please go and quiz them and call me back", I said. Ten minutes later she did just that, issuing an apology and giving me fantastic feedback and appreciation. The mother had realised how much they had learnt: the learning cards had proved a real hit in many ways.

One of the aims of this section is not only to point out the importance of learning, but to show how many variables and options there are, as well as the depth of the learning field. I am only skimming the surface and providing food for thought and a few signposts. You can then decide how long you want to spend on developing learning knowledge, and which direction to take.

There are many factors and facets to consider: what type of learning methods to use, how to help in the acquisition and retention of skills, personal or group preferences, and gender and cultural factors. Other important factors include how much information people can take in, and any learning disorders and disabilities.

Learning is a very interesting and exciting field. Anyone serious about 'learning' needs to spend some time and effort to improve pupils' resources and efficiency.

Having a good grasp of material, complemented with a sound understanding of learning theories for best practice, is a sure way to achieve success in your chosen field. While we play sport for various reasons, some common denominators are to have fun, win and improve. These are all facilitated by learning.

The Seven Learning Styles

It is acknowledged within the field of academic learning that each person has certain preferences when learning. As coaches, we use a mix of styles depending on context and subject, although some people have a dominant style. In one case, after much explaining and physically showing, nothing worked until the pupil continually *watched* me executing the shot. Then they were able to integrate it into their game. Thus, visual learning was the key for this person.

There are numerous ways to describe and note the different ways that people learn. Here is an often-used list of seven learning styles:

- Visual – Using pictures, images and spatial understanding
- Aural – Using sound and hearing

- Verbal – Using words, spoken or written
- Physical – Using body parts, e.g., hands, and the sense of touch
- Logical – Using logic, reasoning and systems
- Social – Using interpersonal interactions, in groups or with other people
- Solitary – Using self-study or learning alone

The important point here is that if you teach or learn in the athlete's preferred style, learning is far more efficient, enjoyable and successful.

In some respects, it is easy to take learning for granted and we generally just pass on what was taught to us. We are creatures of habit, resistant to change and, in many respects, lazy.

A difficulty I face with RACER is *not* getting people to see the efficacy of the concept. This is easily done, but the follow up, the change in behaviour or implementation, is more of a challenge.

In an interview in *The Sunday Telegraph* (January 7, 2020), Professor Paul Dolan says "We are lazy. We don't really change that much about ourselves very often and if we are going to, we need to have a plan, we need to create habits, we need to invest effort into it."

He elaborates more on this aspect of our behaviour in his excellent book *Happiness by Design:* "Your brain is lazy and creates certain habit loops to save you from thinking too hard." The task from my side is to get people to have intentions. What follows is, to use the key phrase academics use, 'the implementation of intentions'.

I have met a number of well known commentators who are really impressed by my RACER pitch, then walk off with a cheery smile. I hear them make the same mistakes the next time I listen to them on television!

Types of Learning Methods and Frameworks

The plethora of research into learning, and the best ways to teach, is increasing year by year. From a 'one-size-fits-all' approach, there is the option of personalised and more targeted learning, especially for more studious and serious players and coaches – as well as a range of theories and ideas to share. Here are just some of the options:

- Open and closed learning – Open learning uses variety and change while a skill is being worked on. Closed learning is a specific task or skill in a defined, set situation.
- Progressive learning – This is when you start with a simple skill and, as mastery improves, the skill becomes more difficult.
- Visualisation – The use of visual images to teach or learn, for example seeing skills in the mind's eye, or physically seeing it.
- Intrinsic and extrinsic – This refers to the motivation of players and coaches. Is a player stimulated by an extrinsic goal such as winning a competition or trophy, or is the intrinsic aim of competing and having pride in one's performance more important?

- Game-based – This is when coaching is taught as isolated skills that come together in a match situation. The idea is to teach within the game itself, perhaps even repeating certain situations.
- Pupil-led approaches – Here the pupil chooses what they want to work on. I recall a Japanese pupil who always turned up with a board upon which he would draw the lesson plan. One week he told me I should beat him 4-0 to finish the lesson – which was no problem for me. Then, one week towards the end of his session (which was being conducted at a peak time), he asked me to play so he could win 4-2. So, at 3-2 to him, in front of watching members, I was running around setting up situations for him to win, while at the same time trying to make the game look natural. On advantage point to my opponent, I set him up with a running-in smash that looks good but should be made most of the time. But he duly won and so off I walked, looking crestfallen at my 'defeat'.

Another very interesting idea is from Russian psychologist Lev Vygotsky. His idea of the Zone of Proximal Development (ZPD) mirrored my thoughts about pushing the pupil at the right level. This means challenging enough to test them, but not too difficult to discourage them.

In fact, an apt perspective on learning comes from Ngakpa Chögyam's excellent book, *Rays Of The Sun: Illustrating Reality*, in which he states that teachers, "must constantly re-express (themselves and knowledge) in terms that are new and fresh, in relation to the situation. They must therefore be sensitive to where they are. They must be sensitive to current conceptual frames of reference – and to the unique nature of people's individual experience."

Beyond Comprehension

I recall an amusing story from one of my university classes about the German philosopher Immanuel Kant. The text was way beyond my range of comprehension. So, when a friend of mine said to the professor, "I don't understand Kant's categorical imperative," my response was: "You lucky bugger!" Yes, it got a good laugh, especially from a few others like me who were at the same 'not even understanding' level.

4. Fun

The more people enjoy what they are doing, the more likely they are to learn and perform better. There is also a strong correlation between retaining people in sport or your classes and whether they are enjoying themselves.

Two examples of children having a great fun time can be seen in the smiling faces in the following shots from one of my coaching sessions.

Mike with smiling students and balls in air

Mike with smiling students and Coach t shirt

Of course, there are exceptions. In Andre Agassi's 2009 best-seller, *Open – an Autobiography*, he comments on how he hated tennis, despite his incredibly successful career.

Fun, the fourth pillar of SELF, embraces many emotions and feelings: enjoyment, amusement, playfulness, good humour, entertainment. Thus, the person in charge has various options for creating the 'fun' factor.

Besides didactic purposes, within the stress of sport and in daily life, humour or light-heartedness can have an important cathartic effect on learning. Studies which emphasise the point include:

- A report in the *College Teaching* journal found that students could recall a statistics lecture more easily when the lecturer added jokes and humour about relevant topics.
- Neurologist Judy Willis has written of how fun increases levels of dopamine, endorphins and oxygen – all things that promote learning.
- In a study for the *Journal of Vocational Behaviour*, Dr Michael J. Tews, Associate Professor at Penn State University, found that employees are more likely to try new things if their work environment is fun.

Having fun while coaching and playing can have a positive impact on learning effectiveness, memory retention, and in promoting self-led or self-guided learning.

Faced with endless, monotonous coaching drills, people can stagnate and become 'bored to death'. Balanced, constructive work within a fun environment is the antidote to this. Achieving the right balance between fun and seriousness is vital.

The Second-Best Coach in the UK

An illustration of the importance of 'fun' happened during a pre-season coaches' camp I was running some years ago. An experienced coach who had run his own academy in Poland applied to work for me. I noticed he was slightly tense and judging by his facial expression, he wasn't engaged in what I thought was pertinent, serious information.

Addressing everyone, but looking at the new coach, I said: "Guys, please listen to what I am saying. We will be using the points I am making now at the summer camps. Besides, what I am saying to you is pertinent and practical, because I am, after all, the UK's second-best coach."

The new coach's expression changed from lack of interest to bewilderment. For the next few minutes his brain went into turmoil as he attempted to resolve some cognitive dissonance after my rather hubristic comment.

Eventually, he could no longer suppress his curiosity and asked: "If you are No.2, who is the No.1 coach in the UK?" I looked at him intensely, straight in the eye. "Actually, I don't know. I want to be modest, so I just say No.2," I remarked. And then, just at the right moment, smiled.

He reacted by falling apart laughing and we all spontaneously reacted likewise. It was a case of making that comment at the right time, place and moment. The point is that after that exchange he listened intently to me and we have been friends and colleagues ever since, for well over a decade.

Using humour to motivate, encourage, learn or deal with situations is indispensable. I am always on the lookout for opportunities to lighten the moment from the intensity of learning and coaching sport. This does not make my type of humour contrived, it is simply an awareness that if you look, you will find the chance to make coaching and learning more fun.

Just When You Think It's Perfect

Teaching your own children any sport is not always easy. I realised this early on with my kids and whenever we went into any teaching situation on the tennis court, we agreed to focus either on coaching or family fun time. The decision had a very positive effect on our personal relationships.

One day I ran a particularly constructive lesson with my son, with no father-son issues disrupting the session. He played amazingly well, and I felt the lesson was well-structured and intense. We both noticed an improvement on all the aspects we worked on and there was a great synthesis of energy.

I complimented my son on his wonderful performance. I then casually asked if he had enjoyed the lesson and he responded: "Dad, it was amazing, but just one question – why do the other kids have so much fun in their lessons?"

This came as a total shock to me and I realised he was right. The intensity and quality were there but there was a lack of fun, which was my responsibility.

To this day, I still ensure there is fun in every one of our sessions.

I do this in a variety of ways, e.g., by playing exciting games after focusing on a shot or skill. For example, if we have worked on his second serve, I may say: "Right, this is the Wimbledon final, you are 30-0 up in the game, 5-4 in the set, but you only have second serves." I then use an enthusiastic voice to hype up the excitement.

Instead of keeping the serious face all the time, I constantly look for the odd quip or something amusing within the context of the situation. For instance, my son may hit a ball just in and I could say: "Bad luck, you just missed the line."

He would respond: "But Dad, that was definitely in!"

I would then reply: "I didn't say it was out, I just said that it had missed the line." So, if that were to happen again, we would both smile and comment with: "Just missed the line, hey?"

This experience was one of the catalysts for making sure fun was part of any coaching dynamic I pursue.

The Alternative 'F' Word

As in RACER's Choice with its hidden Cs, during my research I found in SELF another 'F' besides fun: Forgiveness. I believe that this alternative 'F' is a very important one in many respects. The following stories make my point.

Fun at The Top

Even at the highest performance level, fun applies. Take the England cricket side when they were the No.1 Test team in the world in the early 2010s. By all accounts, they were a happy team.

Star batsman Kevin Pietersen noted about the coaches and management: "These are the kind of guys that make you feel happy when you see them. You'd seek them out at mealtimes. They created the space to have a really enjoyable time playing cricket for England."

When a new coaching and management structure came in, Pietersen reckoned the fun was removed. "We weren't individuals anymore. We were component assets," he said. "If you were enjoying yourself, you were doing something wrong. We were mentally fatigued to the point we were bored with cricket. This stultifying coincided with a drastic decline in performance."

It is fascinating to read why, even at the top levels of sport, striking a balance between fun and striving to be the best is so important.

No-One Is Perfect

An article in *The Times* (26/08/17) by the eloquent and perceptive former England cricket captain Mike Atherton illustrates the importance of forgiveness.

The article was about his former international team-mate, Chris Lewis, who had gone from experiencing the highs and rewards of top-level sport, to the low of being caught trying to import a reported £140,000 worth of cocaine into the UK. He was later given a 13-year prison sentence.

As Atherton's article unfolded, I realised the pain and regret Lewis must have felt. It then struck me how important it is to forgive yourself and your team-mates for mistakes. If we keep battering ourselves, SELF is hampered.

As a young cricket coach, and with my father's connections, I was extremely lucky to chaperone and coach with the amazing Alvin Kallicharran, from the West Indies. At the time, he was one of the world's leading batsmen. He was of Indo-Guyanese ethnicity, and was brought to South Africa to help break down Apartheid barriers.

One day he politely asked me to stop the car. I pulled over and he started to light a cigarette. I was horrified at the spectacle of seeing one of my heroes, and a great of the game, smoking!

He explained to me when (to paraphrase the Supertramp song *Take the Long Way Home*, when you're on stage it's amazing,, but then you come down to earth and ordinary life can be boring. In a way I didn't forgive him for destroying my fantasy of the elite sportsman. Yet on reading Atherton's article it was like a small weight was lifted from my past.

The point here is that this fourth pillar is not only fun but should also include forgiveness.

Sir Alex Does It, "Right after the game"

From a team perspective, forgiveness is vitally important. As angry as you are at a team-mate's unforced error or a golden opportunity missed, the team needs every member to pull in the same direction positively. Forgiving mistakes and forgiving yourself is vital in achieving this, and it is best done sooner rather than later.

As Ferguson notes: "No one likes to get criticised. But in the football dressing room, it's necessary that you point out your players' mistakes. I do it right after the game. I don't wait until Monday, I do it and it's finished. I'm on to the next match. There is no point in criticising a player forever."

As a final note on forgiveness, the following idea is vital:

Do unto yourself as you would unto others.

It's all very well having others treat you with a SELF outlook, but how do you actually relate to yourself?

Many people, including myself, treat others well, i.e., in the context of SELF, but are too harsh on themselves. I once asked a pupil who furiously berated himself whether he would speak to others like that. He looked at me slightly bemused, smiled and took my point. It is a good idea to reflect on this point and to rate yourself in terms of your self-behaviour.

As Brad Gilbert, the former tennis coach to Andre Agassi and Andy Murray, said:

"You already have an opponent on the other side of the net, don't create one on your side."

Be as determined as you want but it is not necessary to abuse and over-berate yourself. Are you as enthusiastic about your efforts and achievements as you would be of others? Are you enthusiastic towards the task at hand and enjoying yourself?

Finally, smile, have fun. I remember playing a squash match against someone and I looked at my face in the bathroom at an interval. I looked like I had been in forced manual labour! "Smile" I said to myself, "have fun and enjoy the game." Post-match my opponent asked me what I had taken during the interval, since my performance level had soared so much.

In Summary

Having observed a great deal of coaching, I am, more than ever, convinced that the fundamentals of SELF, if integrated more into coaches' overall philosophy and psychology, will enhance peoples' quality of experience.

Undoubtedly, the best coaches at all levels will already be using most, if not all these fundamentals. But all coaches could advance their credentials and coaching further by being mindful of creating a Safe environment with an Enthusiastic attitude in which players can Learn while also having Fun.

SELF is a template that will help in any coaching, teaching, learning or relationship environment. I am committed to – and passionate about – this acronym's veracity as a general guide to improving your coaching.

In short, the better the SELF, the better you will be as a coach and a human being.

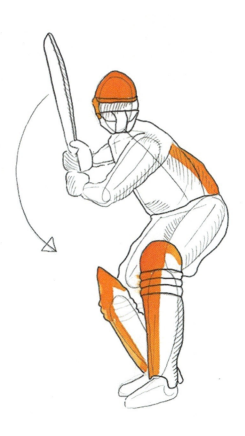

Chapter 7

THE COACH

"Coaching is very complex: it's like a puzzle, and many things need to come together to make it work."

– Stan Wawrinka

My aim in this chapter is to offer coaches more insights, methods and ideas for working with and teaching RACER, and for general readers to have an insight into the coaching world. I intentionally start the chapter by illustrating the importance of the values and respect a coach should have for their pupils. Some of the information may repeat what's been discussed elsewhere, but will suit coaches coming straight to this section, and hopefully provide a memory jolt, clarification or elaboration for those who have read earlier chapters.

Coaches should by now understand the RACER system. The aim now is to find their own best way to practise and train it.

Finding the specific skills and, for coaches, the way to teach the skill, requires thought, innovation, an open mind and experience, plus trial and error. The benefits of this chapter include:

- Improving understanding of RACER
- Demonstrating flexibility and ideas when implementing RACER.
- Creating higher motivation for the coach and pupils
- Increasing the quality of instruction
- Achieving higher satisfaction all-round, which translates to higher income

How My Young Son Became A Man – The Value of The Coach

I have always stressed the vital importance of being a role model to coaches working under my wing, and in general discussions regarding coaches and coaching. This is emphasised in a story about my then 12-year-old son, Jake.

Jake had helped on one of my summer camps, working as one of the drills and games assistants. A group would do technical work and then go over to the drills and games courts. Jake was full of enthusiasm and confidence and was a talented player himself. At the age of eight he was recognised as one of the best players for his age group in the UK, despite competing against 10-year-old opponents. He also got the chance to play Boris Becker and played an incredible point against Tim Henman on a specially constructed court in Trafalgar Square!

Four years later, he was still a young lad and becoming an invaluable asset to the tennis academy. One day, he was working with an eight-year-old pupil of mine called Sam. At the end of the session, Sam's mother came up to me and said: "Mike, I must tell you what happened yesterday after tennis. We were cycling back and someone very young cycled past. The cyclist said, "Hi, Sam".

"With a huge smile and full of admiration, my Sam shouted back, "Hi Jake!" He was so happy and excited, so I asked him: "Who was that?"

"Sam replied: "Mum, that's the man taking us for tennis." When his father arrived home and asked how the tennis lesson had gone, Sam's first response was: "Dad, the man teaching us cycled right past us and said hello to me.""

This illustrates the respectful light in which young pupils may see their coach. Thus, the responsibility and effort that coaches make should then be commensurate with this high esteem they are valued with.

Modern Coaching

"The whole reason I moved to the US to be coached by Alberto Salazar is to be able to improve one to two percent. I was sick of coming sixth in the world, seventh in the world, and getting close to a medal, but not quite there, half a second."

– Mo Farah

The importance of a good coach to any casual, amateur or professional player is undisputed, as noted previously, for many reasons. Backed by the Internet revolution and motivated by an increasingly competitive world, pupils have become more discerning and knowledgeable. Their leisure time is increasingly more precious, creating more demanding checks and qualification requirements for coaches.

To compete, today's coaches must continually improve on aspects of their coaching. RACER, in conjunction with SELF, are the ideal tools to achieve this aim.

Making Gains – Maximum, And Marginal

Coaches with aspirations to improve should always be on the lookout for 'marginal gains', the often overlooked, small details that can be the difference between success and failure, victory or defeat. Obviously, I hope the improvement from RACER is not marginal, but that it will make a fundamental change to people's perceptions and performance.

Forget the Lesson, Someone Actually Greeted Us!

I once took a call from a parent whose child had wanted to move to my academy. After our first introductory session, and with the family in tow, I went to introduce myself and ask how they thought the session had gone.

The mother told me that before they walked onto court, her family and child were already won over. They had been warmly greeted at the entrance by one of my assistants. Then a coach, who didn't know the child, greeted them and struck up a conversation while walking to the next class. The lady told me her child had been nervous and apprehensive before but due to the warm greetings was smiling just before they went on court.

She expressed her sincere gratitude and then, almost as an after-thought, said: "Oh, by the way, the lesson was great." The mother stressed how wonderful and different the experience had been compared to the cold, machine-like operation they had attended before.

Communication is key from the start. Any advantage or improvement in the skills a coach gains will benefit the coach, as well as the people they interact with.

> *SELF is the basis of a good coach, the indispensable hard drive. RACER*
> *is the software, giving a wide variety of practical options.*

Each situation is different, and a synergy that arises between the parties ultimately determines their success, or otherwise. The story below stresses the importance of personalising coaching.

"Dad, I Have A New Name"

One of the perks of my job has been to see my own kids in classes with my other coaches, as well as having the opportunity to teach them myself. Then, latterly, to watch them coach and receive wonderful compliments and feedback about them.

One summer's day, after my daughter, Rachael, had been at one of our camps as an attendee, I asked her how the session had gone. Watching from a distance, it had looked pretty good. "Dad, it was such fun. We focused on the forehand and the serve. And I have a new name now."

"What do you mean?" I asked.

"Well, every time it was my turn, the coach looked at me and said,

"Next". So now I think my name is 'Next.'" Being astute, Rachael had picked up the impersonal nature of the communication.

In a coaches' meeting the next morning, besides reviewing the day ahead I addressed the issue of speaking to pupils. In short, the word 'next' to address a pupil whose chance it was, was to all intents and purposes banned. Rather, eye contact, name and positive comments were to be the emphasis.

Some coaches get so caught up in the sport itself, and the winning and losing that the personal connection can be lost. Nurturing the human touch has been one of the reasons for my success in coaching.

Teaching RACER

There is no one set method for how to teach the RACER system. There could be many people who have better implementations for it than me, or who find better paths and methods in teaching it.

Rocket Science

While I try not to overuse the term 'keep it simple', there are many aspects of coaching and playing whereby with less complexity and solid basics in place we can go quite far.

This perception was reinforced by the British tennis Davis Cup-winning captain, Leon Smith. Having been chosen to be part of the Lawn Tennis Association's Davis Cup Legacy programme, I had the opportunity to learn from him, and quiz him.

When asked what he thought the top-ranked players were doing in training – was it amazing drills or sophisticated sports science work – the answer was simple. Basically, nothing out of the ordinary that a good, experienced coach doesn't already do with their pupils. But the quality, effort and intensity are the key difference with elite performers.

Coaches must remember how important the basics are, as the following story illustrates.

> ## "Watch the Ball! Now Let's Go Grab A Damn Drink!"
>
> How many times does a coach or parent say to their pupil or child: "Watch the ball!" This is probably the most overused expression in ball sports.
>
> My own tennis coach once attended a John McEnroe practice session and observed and questioned aspects of his game. Did he have enough racket rotation on the backswing of his forehand? On the volley, was he using his fingers enough to get the required backspin, not palming the ball?
>
> If you watch clips of McEnroe volleying, it is far from a traditional technique. My coach watched Mac's ground reaction force, i.e., the power we get when pushing off the ground, and it looked good. Viewing this, he wondered what intricacy or detail the world No.1's coach would be enlightening his charge with? So, with ears wide open and pen at the ready, he watched as the coach called time on the session and McEnroe approached him.
>
> "So, coach, what can you tell me?" asked Mac. The coach looked him straight in the eye and responded: "Mac, how many times have I told you, just watch the bloody ball! Let's go grab a damn drink."

We all need to focus on the basics. After all, we are playing the same game as the champions. They may look impressive but when it comes down to it, we can also pull off incredible plays and have moments of genius, beyond our regular level. When we have that wonderful moment, we feel like a pro. It's a superb feeling, one of the great thrills of sport.

I do need to add that while 'watch the ball' is a correct and sometimes necessary coaching reminder, RACER takes it a step further: it encourages us to Anticipate the ball and not only rely on eyesight. I am known to comment that watching the ball onto your racket, foot or into your hands, is too late. As coaches, we need to be coaching the tracking of the ball.

Sometimes, what should rather be said is 'Anticipate,' because without this skill, it can be very difficult to 'watch the ball'.

The Pillars Of RACER

Before discussing the three major approaches to teaching RACER, one dilemma has to be resolved. Do you inform your pupils of RACER, or not? It is perfectly feasible to work on any aspect without your pupils being aware of the fact they are working within – and being taught – the RACER system, or any system. In other words, RACER can simply be integrated into day-to-day coaching.

For example, you work on their Ready positions. Spend time on Anticipation. Have some sessions where Choice can be discussed and practiced. As noted, most coaches cover all these areas at some point. Top athletes utilise RACER principles because a well-applied RACER system is how most good performances arise. This may be done without specific reference to a system, if structured so that the system helps, rather than an arbitrary teaching of the elements.

If you'd prefer your pupils not to think about the system, and you can see improvement in both your coaching abilities and the players' performance and outcome, then, in fact, there is no argument. It is 100 percent acceptable that just the coach is aware of this structure.

Nevertheless, the information that follows is still essential to the coach, who perhaps feels that their players will overthink and thus not perform processes naturally. In my opinion, there are more advantages than disadvantages to informing the players of the system. Yet the degree to which you make the system conscious or subconscious is optional.

Thanks to RACER, as I already noted, I discovered areas to work on that I hadn't put enough emphasis on before. I traced the root of errors, dealing with causes and not effects. My enthusiasm for coaching increased further, and my interest after over 30 years in coaching was given a lift. My own tennis also improved, which was another great sign of the efficacy of RACER.

Most importantly, my pupils picked up on my enthusiasm and were excited by something innovative and different.

Teaching RACER

I must re-emphasise that RACER is not a rigid, inflexible dogma. The system is very pliable, and it is also very empirical. You observe or play your chosen sport, and then see how RACER fits in. I am confident you will find that it does.

There is no single, definitive way to impart the RACER system, and there are numerous factors to consider:

- The specific pupils, or team and individuals within a team
- Time of teaching, if one has a periodisation programme
- Weather
- Match planning
- Post-match work
- Your knowledge and personality, and what you are comfortable with, in terms of getting the principles across

Much depends on the work and effort that the coach wants to put into developing themselves, implementing and exploring RACER.

Look at one of the greatest football coaches of this century, Jose Mourinho. He served first in the professional game as an interpreter for Bobby Robson at FC Porto and Sporting Lisbon in his Portuguese homeland. He then enjoyed numerous stints as an assistant coach, observing, writing and learning, as well as following Robson to Barcelona, initially.

Mourinho's search for knowledge, improvement and perfection resulted in his rise to be the manager of one of the world's biggest clubs, Manchester United, in 2016. One can safely say that he had the determination and motivation, and was willing to give the proverbial blood, sweat and tears that are required. This does not mean everyone has to do this, but that is the benchmark.

The RACER system gives you something different and can instil confidence in your pupils. It also shows those being taught that you are going the extra mile. It adds something new to your lessons with the additional benefit that people will want more of what you can provide, so you are more likely to be recommended and in demand.

To achieve this, be aware that improvements can be based on a combination of core principles and personality factors:

- Developing knowledge and being willing to learn more about any – and all – aspects of your sport.
- Attitude – Improving your approach and patience when it comes to pupils' progress, and their individual personalities.
- Communication – How do you impart your message? Do you use stories, humour or good analogies and anecdotes? Remember, a whisper can penetrate deeper than a booming voice, a raised eyebrow usually says more than a shouted command.
- Care – Pupils pick up on how much a coach cares and are generally aware of their emotional state and attitude. They subconsciously read body language, verbal and facial expressions, and their overall demeanor or 'vibe'.
- Teaching skills – Do you use good progressions? Don't forget 'show and tell', which is always a good combo.

As coaches, we should always be mindful of our conduct, personality, appearance, experience, patience and enthusiasm.

Causes and Effects

RACER not only gives the coach a systematic checklist to improve performance, but crucially, it outlines the basic order of all actions in sport. It reminds us that there are causes behind the results we are achieving.

Thus, there's little benefit in asking someone to Anticipate better if they aren't in the correct Ready position. Similarly, there is less efficacy in asking someone to improve their Execution if, in fact, they have made a poor Choice. And, while we can always make the best Choice and thus the subsequent Execution can be corrected, the player or team needs to be made aware when the best Choice wasn't made. RACER opens our understanding of causes and effects and raises the bar of our coaching repertoires.

Options for Learning

When I thought about and have taught RACER over the years, three distinct methods for teaching the latter seem to have become clear. While the three are not mutually exclusive, they can be distinct enough to give both coaches and players a definite, specific option.

Understanding these three possibilities will add to coaches' knowledge and depth of RACER, as well as giving flexibility in providing different ideas on how to impart the concept.

The Three RACER Teaching Methods:

1. Teaching the RACER elements in sequence
2. Linking the RACER elements
3. Using the RACER elements in a variable way

Let's look at each of these in turn.

1. Teaching RACER Elements in Sequence

The coach teaches or improves each element, in RACER's sequential order. The coach does a check, clarification or thorough analysis and training of each of the elements, one at a time. This continues until pupils or players are aware of and have practised relatively sufficiently to move onto the next element. A sequential analysis would proceed as follows:

- Are they Ready physically, tactically and mentally? Are they in the right position, and in a positive and calm mindset?
- Anticipation – Being aware of what team-mates are doing, what the opponent is doing. Using their senses, especially the eyes.
- Choice – Reaffirm that all players will be deciding, a definite and irrevocable Choice. Either ask your pupils to be aware they are making a Choice and focus on the concept or mix their Choices up.
- Choice entails defence, neutral and attack. There are subdivisions here as well. A numerical scale is also good to use, such as: '1' is desperate defence and '10' is borderline defence.
- It's important to make pupils aware of Choice as a concept. Then perhaps ask them to use more of one option than another so they are practising Choice.
- Execution – Both psychological and technical. Are they staying in the moment, having the correct thought at the right time? Is the mind focused? Is the player Executing the correct way? Concentrate on performance rather than outcome, and what can be controlled, rather than what they can't control.
- Finally, Recover. Get up and get moving back to your best Ready position as efficiently and quickly as possible. Coaches often focus on the Execution, but don't spend enough time on psychological and physical Recovery work. While these are taught in sequence, you could ostensibly start with, say, Choice first before moving onto Execution.

2. Linking the RACER Elements

The next teaching method is to use combinations of RACER's five elements, instead of working on each aspect individually. The RACER combos give a powerful and dynamic boost to any coach or player. The essentials are:

Ready – Anticipate
Anticipate – Choice
Choice – Execute
Execute – Recover
Recover – Ready

Let's look at each combination.

Ready – Anticipate

Work on the Ready position, followed by how quickly you can Anticipate and get into the correct position for your shot.

So, in badminton, be in the correct Ready position to receive, serve and Anticipate if the server is doing a tap or a high one over your head, for instance. You may have to stand in a more forward or back Ready position, based on your Anticipation of your opponent's serve.

In boxing, you maintain your correct stance and watch your opponent's eyes to Anticipate their next move, with your peripheral vision on their gloves. You need to be pretty good at this combo, otherwise you won't be able to practice it for too long – you'll be lying prone on the floor.

Anticipate – Choice

When working on Anticipation, you can combine it with Choice. Work on Anticipation and follow this by becoming mindful of Choice – and then practice making some actual Choices.

For example, if you are practising the steal from an opponent's lineout in rugby union, watch the thrower's eyes to see if you can pick up any cues. Anticipate and watch their every movement, including arm speed as they throw in the ball. If you can pick up any cues or clues, your Choice of when to jump will be improved, and your chances of stealing the ball will be enhanced.

In the 2020 NBA finals, one of the deciding factors was the "stealing or rebound recovery" of the ball by Anthony Davies of the Lakers. He anticipated the shot and made his Choice and moved to jump precisely and better than the defenders who outnumbered him.

Choice – Execution

I see coaches in racket sports working on technical Execution, but have they examined Choice? The coach shows the pupil how to hit or Execute but often, no specific Choice is involved. The result is an unclear idea of exactly what the aim of the Execution is.

For example, a new pupil comes to me with a problem with their forehand. They complain of being inconsistent and missing too many easy shots closer to the net. As we play, I observe that they have very good shape when hitting for the back of the court. But I also notice that they use the same Execution from close to the net, and with a similar swing, no matter how fast I hit the ball.

While, of course, Anticipation is involved, the point is that my pupil was not making clear Choices. I then showed the Choices involved, relative to their level such as deciding to go higher and slower when out of position, or to play a lower shot when close to the net. By working on the Choice and Execute combination, soon enough the pupil's so-called problem was barely there.

Execute – Recover

I have already mentioned how people in serving sports, and cricket bowlers practicing in the nets, for example, mostly work on their Execution. So, by emphasising the connection here, players focus on the Execution and Recovery. A bowler will work more intensely on trying to catch a return shot from the batsman rather than only working on the bowling Execution.

A great example of this is Jofra Archer, the new England cricket star dropping the world's leading Test batsman, Steve Smith, in this way in the 2019 Ashes. I believe more awareness and trying in this area will make a difference.

Ready – Recover: The Two Rs

The Ready and Recover link is worth stressing. As a teacher, I generally start with 'The Two Rs' because invariably, being Ready explicitly requires Recovering.

Ready and Recover form the core of the RACER concept. They are the shell that keeps the RACER idea secure and effective (R-ACE-R). If you are always Ready and you Recover from what you do, the 'ACE', the core of the concept, has a far better chance of success.

The Two Rs are often a great way to begin a session, as the emphasis is more on movement and preparedness, rather than the more complex ACE actions.

3. Variable Use of RACER Elements

The final method of teaching RACER is learning to mix and match. You can combine any elements in any way you wish. Thus, you may decide to work on Ready and keeping a good shape to your Execution. Or you could work on good Anticipation and feeling mental freedom on your Execution.

You could be aware of making a Choice and make sure Recovery is efficient, or Execute and make sure you are Ready. This shows how fluid and open the RACER system is. While the main sequence of RACER remains, there are twists, turns and overlaps.

So, while Anticipation essentially happens when someone is Executing something, in fact, you also start Anticipating after you have Executed. Thus, in any sport, if you hit a good shot you are already Anticipating a defensive play from your opponent, so you may take up an aggressive Ready position.

Or, if you are attacked from an Execution, you are expecting pressure from your opponents and thus may play safe, as you are already Anticipating trouble before you have even Executed.

After watching your players, you might encourage them to Recover better. Perhaps you feel their Anticipation as a group is leading to poor teamwork, so you work on 'Team Anticipation'.

In football, if you notice headers in the middle third of the pitch that show ball retention is poor, then you can show how, by Anticipating better movement, your team is more likely to win or retain possession. The ball can only be headed so far within a certain range, and some areas more likely than others. So, the players in your team should be moving in an area where you can retain the ball. This is based on evidence watching Manchester United live (2014-2017). I was amazed how such a high-quality side lost or didn't win possession in this heading situation.

Finally, possibly work on the different Executions, in high risk and low risk situations. Do this without pressure, then add as much pressure as possible whether this be in defence, neutral or attacking situations.

In teaching or coaching RACER, it is very important to understand that having the correct thought at the correct time is vital. If your mind is thinking of the outcome after Executing you may not Recover properly, so your thoughts are not in the right order.

Or, if you should be Choosing then Executing and you are so busy with your Choice that you are still thinking about it when you Execute, this will affect your Execution.

If you are thinking of the outcome or what will happen rather than just Execution, your thoughts are again in the wrong order.

Many mistakes in sport are made because the person gets the wrong thought at the wrong time. When they should be focusing on a specific object, their mind is thinking about something else.

People in winning positions start thinking about victory rather than the correct next thought. Instead of focusing on catching the ball and then the pass, the thought goes too quickly to the pass and the ball is dropped.

The Brain Surgeons' Wives – Amazing Neurological Discovery

I was teaching two doctors whose husbands were brain surgeons. Every week, they couldn't get the hang of a coordination exercise I was trying to get them to do as part of their warm-up. We joked that we may need to get one of their husbands in for a bit of cerebral re-wiring, and had fun deciding who should perform it.

Then, one week, one of them said the inability to grasp the exercise had become embarrassing and that I needed to give them a tip. So, I thought deeply, realised I had given conventional instructions such as "watch the ball, don't rush". Yet the mistakes they were making were not so much about coordination but thought organisation, i.e., arranging their thoughts so they could Execute better.

So, after coaching on that day I practically set about trying to work out the solution. What was the order of thoughts they should be having as, in fact, it was not an overly difficult exercise? Then I got it, I had the right order of thoughts. I tested it on some people who hadn't done it before and my instructions worked.

The next week when they turned up for their lesson my smile gave it all away. I gave them two instructions to follow and they did it, and to their great joy and excitement the problem was solved. I subsequently coined the term **thought sequencing**.

An amazing example of this happened during the third Ashes Test of 2019 noted earlier in the book. With England nine wickets down and needing two runs to win their No. 11 batsman, Jack Leach, was stranded out of his crease and the Australian bowler, Nathan Lyon, only had to catch the ball thrown in from the fielder and take off the bails to give Australia victory.

But his thoughts, instead of focusing on Executing the catch first, instead went to breaking the bails. He duly fumbled the ball and that chance of immediate victory was gone; the wrong thought at the wrong time or, as I say, incorrect thought sequencing.

I recommend that you do the following exercise before you read on. It's good for your coordination and shows how thought patterns can – or don't – work. If you do the exercise correctly, your thoughts are in the correct sequence, and vice versa.

Testing and Practising Thought Sequencing

Hit a ball slowly up in the air with your right hand. Take the racket behind your back and put it into your left hand. Meanwhile, the ball bounces, that's good. Now hit the ball up in the air with your left hand and then take it behind your back, then back into your right hand, and so on. If possible, do the exercise before reading on.

Nine out of ten get it wrong and pass the racket in front of them and then behind their backs, hitting with the same hand twice.

I discovered what the problem was. The thinking order must be specific and in order. It goes as follows:

- Watch the ball as you softly hit it up into the air with your right hand, but then do not think about the ball.
- Concentrate on taking the racket back behind your back into your left hand.
- Focus on tapping the ball up with your left hand, and don't think about the ball.
- Then say: "Racket behind the back and change into your right hand again", etc.

I have had people doing this exercise for many years, and nearly everyone fails until they listen and follow the instructions to have the right thought at the right time, i.e., thought sequencing.

This applies to so much of our coaching and teaching and, if used appropriately, will make an impressive difference to your pupils and coaching.

Thinking ahead is part of Anticipation, but it is vital to remember that we primarily stay in the moment, present and fully conscious of what is happening in our minds and bodies. Here are a few examples:

- Celebrating or becoming overconfident before you win is often a recipe for disaster. It shows your thoughts are not focused on the task at hand. Again, it's about having the wrong thought at the wrong time.
- One of the major reasons why individuals or teams lose late in the game is that the mind begins to lose clarity of thought when the body is tired.

- A fielder in cricket or baseball comes running in to throw the ball and run the batsman or hitter out. The temptation is for the mind to jump ahead to skittling the stumps, as noted in the Nathan Lyon example earlier, or in the case of baseball, to Executing a winning throw to third base, before picking up the ball cleanly. Thinking beyond the present task at hand may result in a fumble and a chance being missed.

Essential Coaching Skills And RACER

After 40 years of coaching, I thought it would be a good idea to include just a few of the excellent ideas I have developed or come across from many coaching courses. RACER can be used, or not, in all the situations that follow here.

Creativity

I remember as a young coach being horrified when the children in a tennis lesson asked me to play a certain game, and I had no idea what it was. So, I subtly got them to play it their way. Basically, it involves the pupils running from tramline to tramline while the coach rolls balls to try and hit them. They called it 'Space Invaders' and I played this for 10 years. Then one day it dawned on me that this game can be played in different ways. Today I have over 40 variations – and I am still adding. The variations add fun, coordination, fitness and ball skills. Oh, and we have given it a new name: 'Rotten Eggs'.

Mike playing Rotten Eggs

The point is, many coaches get shown games or drills and it's useful to be creative by adding and modifying games to add interest, offer a different focus, and test a variety of skills. Using RACER can change a game as you focus on something different. So instead of just doing a usual drill, you could say: "Same drill as usual, guys, but let's be more aware of the Choice before we Execute rather than going through the motions." One can add new variations as well as different scoring. Getting the balance between repetition and change is vital. I urge coaches to be aware and see creativity as an essential skill in coaching.

Dynamic Active Coaching

RACER can be used in any potential situation in sport. Just adding one different element can turn an ordinary drill into a focused, learning experience.

So much time, enthusiasm and concentration are lost by people hanging around during coaching sessions doing nothing. The record waiting time I have seen is a group of tennis pupils at a club I happened to be observing. Part of a group of 12, each one waited 18 minutes for a chance to hit a ball. I've seen waiting while lining up to practise a penalty in football, or being part of a circle while a rugby ball is thrown around. I hear and see too many of these stories and there is no excuse for it – particularly in a climate such as the UK's during the cold winter months.

Personally, I didn't start off with such dynamic interactive coaching. It soon became apparent to me that to maximise value, learning, practise and enjoyment for pupils it was necessary to keep them busy and working. Of course, one tempers the work-rate accordingly on a boiling hot day.

Divide the players into smaller, practical groups, whatever the skill level. Get as many people as possible to be actively doing something, whether passing, kicking or catching. In some sports such as tennis, which is highly technical, adequate Execution explanation time is needed, so set up some activities on the outside of the main activity area for pupils who aren't immediately engaged. Footwork skills, shadowing skills, movement and stretching are some activities which can keep pupils engaged throughout. The photo below shows an example of the footwork skills the pupils will be working on, while the coach will be, for example, working on the technique of others.

Mike with kids and cones back view

A high level of dynamism is not difficult with a bit of forethought. To be good at maintaining it takes time and practise, but this will be appreciated by your pupils.

Game Situation Coaching – Make It Real

I have watched so many training sessions where too much time is used up with unrealistic exercises like running in and shooting at an open goal. Or just hitting the ball back and forth with no apparent purpose.

Sometimes these exercises are necessary, but too often coaches don't improve on the initial idea, choosing to use it to fill in time. For example, why not have a defender blocking your path even if there is no serious intent to win the ball in the first instance, then get the player to shoot at goal? I see goalkeeping practise with no one between the keeper and the kicker. How often does this clear vision happen in a match situation?

After All's Said and Done... Maybe Not

There is more to the role of a coach than just concentrating on the sport itself. We play sport for many personal and psychological reasons. The coach plays a vital part in helping to improve people's lives through the sporting process, but we also play it to improve our lives.

James Blake, the American former top-10 tennis player, writing in his 2007 autobiography *Breaking Back: How I Lost Everything and Won Back My Life*, noted that his coach spent 50 percent of the time talking generally about life and psychology outside of the sport, and the positive effect that this had on him.

Matthew Syed, the award-winning sportswriter, wrote of how impressed he was with Saracens rugby union club, who were "trying to stretch their players, to develop them not just as rugby players, but as leaders. They are a club who want young men capable of using their own initiative." Their aim was to develop decent human beings on and off the field.

I recall a coach watching me teach in South Africa in the 1980s, commenting that I was overdoing it. According to him, there was no way I could continue at that pace and level of energy. By sheer coincidence, he saw me coaching in London 30 years later. He literally walked onto court, apologised to the pupil, reintroduced himself to me and just said that it was unbelievable I was still coaching with the same intensity and tempo three decades later. The point is not arrogance, but a commitment to pupils, and the pride in the profession.

RACER can add to enjoyment while at the same time being constructive in team games. Instead of, "Okay, let's play a game", it's, "Okay, let's play a game and be aware of your Anticipation, your Choices", or whatever instruction the coach intends.

In Summary

More than 40 years of coaching experience gives me the confidence to believe that just about any coach at whatever level should be able to benefit from at least some of the insights, ideas and suggestions in this chapter.

I have elaborated on the different ways of coaching RACER, while at the same time broadening your understanding of the system. I've tried to stress the importance of creativity, dynamism and having fun with your pupils.

I am not arrogant enough to think that I, too, don't need to improve and learn from others, but I do believe that I have made a major contribution to coaching development through RACER and the ideas that are outlined in SELF. I hope you agree and that you find them useful.

2020 Photo of kids with balls in the air

Appendix

CHARTING

There are several reasons why you would use charting. Charts help to measure progress or not, and can guide learning or learning goals. They can be an exceptionally powerful motivator for practise, to make you work harder, and can boost confidence. The charts can be as specific or general as you wish. So you can, in effect, draw up a chart for your own requirements.

The charts are all based around the RACER system, and I have kept them relatively basic. Thus, while you can chart your general Readiness you can also break this down into detail, e.g., after a success or failure. From a specific situation, such as a corner, tackle, return of serve, under stress or fatigue, does your dynamic Readiness decrease in proficiency after a failure? On a personal and professional level, I have found charts very useful on all the accounts mentioned above.

If you, for some reason, don't use charts, at least keep a chart in your mind of your pupil's level in each of the five RACER elements. I have, over the years, developed a photographic memory of my pupils' RACER skills and thus often, and for other reasons not relevant here, don't use charts for all my pupils.

The rollercoaster nature of sports performance and outcomes often fluctuates, sometimes beyond your control, perhaps dramatically. Throw in a bit of Lady Luck and the relative nature of measurement must be considered.

Thus, the charts need to be used and analysed intelligently, to assess and obtain the most important and relevant charting information. Consider having 70 percent possession in a field sport and you lose the game 3-0. What's the point of that information? How do you then use that knowledge to access and assess core reasons for defeat?

Charting the work information is also known as data analysis, or looking more forensically at all the relevant angles to get the most pertinent information. You can use the book's charts as is, or as a guide to draw your own version, using the RACER system to see if it helps you start achieving your goals. The system I use is '1' for a low level, sliding up to excellence at '10'.

As an additional extra I have also added the SELF chart at the end of this section to help map your progress. When I charted my personal SELF I realised I was teaching too much, so my score was low on the learning ('L') side, even though there was great content and information being presented. Of course, on fun my score was through the roof! Happy charting, and (pre-) congratulations on your improvement.

Styling in Switzerland

I recall being in Switzerland some years back to take a tennis qualification. The head instructor turned up while I was practicing with a fellow participant. He watched, and then said: "Mike, your style is fantastic."

The smile on my face was stretched wide, until he commented:

"It's just a shame about your feet."

In a course discussion later, the instructor referred to his sharp quip and explained how easy it is, and how most coaches don't have to move their feet too often as they can get away with good shots or by just saying, "Good shot."

This affected me very positively and I then drew up a chart just for my general Ready position. As my charting became more specific, I realised my Ready position for my serve could be better as I wasn't pushing powerfully off the ground enough for wide balls. So, I set an aim and the charting not only set me in the right direction but motivated me to improve. The overall result was not only a definite improvement in my Ready position, but in a specifically weaker area of my game as well.

Charting Examples:

Ready

Rating	Day 1	Day 2	Day 3	Day 4	Day 5	Day 6	Day 7	Notes
10								
9								
8								
7								
6								
5								
4								
3								
2								
1								

Remember, your Ready chart can and should also focus on more specific Ready aspects. Refer to Chapter 1 on Ready and this will give valuable pointers as to the many different charts that can be created for improving your personal, and your team's Ready state.

Charting Examples:

Ready

Rating	Day 1	Day 2	Day 3	Day 4	Day 5	Day 6	Day 7	Notes
10								
9								
8								
7								
6								
5								
4								
3								
2								
1								

Anticipation

Rating	Day 1	Day 2	Day 3	Day 4	Day 5	Day 6	Day 7	Notes
10								
9								
8								
7								
6								
5								
4								
3								
2								
1								

Charting Examples:

Anticipation

Rating	Day 1	Day 2	Day 3	Day 4	Day 5	Day 6	Day 7	Notes
10								
9								
8								
7								
6								
5								
4								
3								
2								
1								

Choice

Rating	Day 1	Day 2	Day 3	Day 4	Day 5	Day 6	Day 7	Notes
10								
9								
8								
7								
6								
5								
4								
3								
2								
1								

Charting Examples:

Choice

Rating	Day 1	Day 2	Day 3	Day 4	Day 5	Day 6	Day 7	Notes
10								
9								
8								
7								
6								
5								
4								
3								
2								
1								

Execution

Rating	Day 1	Day 2	Day 3	Day 4	Day 5	Day 6	Day 7	Notes
10								
9								
8								
7								
6								
5								
4								
3								
2								
1								

Charting Examples:

Execution

Rating	Day 1	Day 2	Day 3	Day 4	Day 5	Day 6	Day 7	Notes
10								
9								
8								
7								
6								
5								
4								
3								
2								
1								

Recovery

Rating	Day 1	Day 2	Day 3	Day 4	Day 5	Day 6	Day 7	Notes
10								
9								
8								
7								
6								
5								
4								
3								
2								
1								

Charting Examples:

Recovery

Rating	Day 1	Day 2	Day 3	Day 4	Day 5	Day 6	Day 7	Notes
10								
9								
8								
7								
6								
5								
4								
3								
2								
1								

SELF Chart:

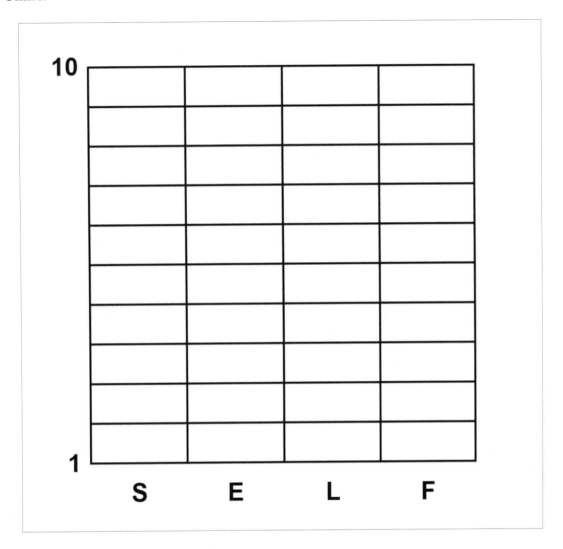

BIBLIOGRAPHY

Agassi, A., *Open: An Autobiography*, Harper Collins, 2009.

Atherton, Mike. *Mike Atherton meets Chris Lewis: 'That first night in jail… I had a plan to tie my sheets together'*, The Times, 2017.

Burwash, P., *Tennis for Life*, Times Books, 1981. Chögyam, N., *Rays of the Sun: Illustrating Reality*, Aro Books Worldwide. 2011.

Coakley, J. & Dunning, E., *Handbook Of Sports Studies*, Sage Publications Ltd, 2000.

Collina P., *The Rules Of The Game*, Pan, 2004.

Cox, R., *Sports Psychology: Concepts And Applications*, McGraw-Hill Education, 2011.

Dolan, P., *Happiness By Design: Finding Pleasure and Purpose in Everyday Life*, Penguin, 2014.

Ferguson, A., *Managing My Life*, Hodder & Stoughton, 2000. Fox, A., *Think To Win: The Strategic Dimension Of Tennis*, Harper Collins, 1993.

Gallwey. T. W., *The Inner Game of Tennis – The ultimate guide to the mental side of peak performance*, Pan, 2015.

Gilbert, B. & and Jamison, S., *Winning Ugly*, Simon & Schuster UK, 2007.

Gladwell, M., *The Tipping Point: How Little Things Can Make A Big Difference*, Abacus, 2002.

Gladwell, M., *Blink: The Power Of Thinking Without Thinking*, Penguin, 2005.

Gretzky, W. and Reilly, R., *Gretzky: An Autobiography*, Harper Collins, 1990.

Kaye, M., *Goal Setting: Goals & Motivation: Introduction To A Complete & Proven Step-By-Step Blueprint For Reaching Your Goals*, MK Coaching, 2016.

Keller, G & Papasan, J., *The ONE Thing: The Surprisingly Simple Truth Behind Extraordinary Results*, John Murray, 2013.

Knight, P., *Shoe Dog: A Memoir By The Creator Of NIKE*, Simon & Schuster UK, 2016.

Knight, S., *NLP at Work: The Essence of Excellence (People Skills for Professionals)*, Nicholas Brealey Publishing, 2009.

Lipschitz, M., Four Pillars to Improve Your Coaching, *British Tennis Coaches Association*, 2011.

Magee, M., *Madness at the Cup Final: The Enduring Tragedy of Paul Gascoigne*, VICE Sports, 2016.

Martens, R., *Successful Coaching*, Human Kinetics, 2012.

Martin, E., *The Dreams of a Champion: Goal Setting Workbook for Peak Performance in Sports and Exercise*, MK Coaching, 2016.

Meurisse, T., *The One Goal: Master the Art of Goal Setting, Win Your Inner Battles, And Achieve Exceptional Results*, CreateSpace Independent Publishing Platform, 2017.

Morris, M., *Goal Setting: 10 Easy Steps To Keep Motivated & Master Your Personal Goals (Goal Setting, Smart Goals,*
and How To Set Goals), CreateSpace Independent Publishing Platform, 2014.

Reid, P., *Cheer Up Peter Reid*, Trinity Mirror Sport Media, 2017.

Seles, M., *Getting A Grip: On My Body, My Mind, My Self*, Avery, 2009.

Sutton, J. & Stewart, W., *Learning To Counsel, 4th Edition: How to Develop the Skills, Insight and Knowledge to Counsel Others*, Robinson, 2017.

Tews, M.J., Michel, J.W. & Noe, R.A., *Does Fun Promote Learning? The Relationship Between Fun in the Workplace and Informal Learning*, Journal of Vocational Behavior, 2016.

Tuhovsky, I., *Zen: Beginner's Guide: Happy, Peaceful and Focused Lifestyle for Everyone (Buddhism, Meditation, Mindfulness, Success)*, CreateSpace Independent Publishing Platform, 2014.

Tyers, A. *The Mike Costello Way to Talk a Good Fight: BBC Broadcaster's Advice for Budding Commentators*, The Daily Telegraph, 2017.

Vickers, J. N., *Perception, Cognition, and Decision Training: The Quiet Eye in Action*. Human Kinetics Europe Ltd, 2007.

Walsh, D., *Appointment of Gareth Southgate Pays Off*, The Times, 2017.

Woodward, C., *Winning! The Path to Rugby World Cup Glory*, Hodder, 2005.